A Ministry that saves Lives

Sermons and Thoughts on Ministry in a Challenging Context

Published by ACB Ministry @ Bethlehem Missionary Baptist Church
Richmond, CA

A MINISTRY THAT SAVES LIVES:
Sermons and Thoughts on Ministry in a Challenging Context

by Alvin C. Bernstine

Foreword by
Dr. J. Alfred Smith, Sr.

2012 by Alvin C. Bernstine

Front Cover Photos: Thinkstock

Published by ACB Ministry @ Bethlehem Missionary Baptist Church, 684 Juliga Woods Street, Richmond, CA 94804

Dedicate to the memory of all the Pastors who like
my predecessor and academic benefactor,
The Reverend Dr. Abraham Henry Newman,
who rose to the challenge of doing ministry in
Richmond, California, a challenging context.

ASHAY!

CONTENTS

FOREWORD 9

ACKNOWLEDGEMENT 11

PREFACE 13

Chapter 1 APPRECIATING THE VALUE OF BLACK LIFE: *A Community Response to the Senseless Killing in the Black Community* 19

Chapter 2 A MINISTRY THAT SAVES LIVES: *Stepping Up* 25

Chapter 3 A MINISTRY THAT SAVES LIVES: *Speaking Up* 35

Chapter 4 A MINISTRY THAT SAVES LIVES: *Giving Up* 47

Chapter 5 HELPING YOUR HOMETOWN: *Ministry with a Focus* 59

Chapter 6 MAKES ME WANNA HOLLER.................... 67

Chapter 7 THE POLITICS OF KILLING STREETS.... 77

Chapter 8 THE MINISTRY OF COFFIN STOPPING...................................... 81

Chapter 9 A MINISTRY FOR PEOPLE LIVING BELOW THE BAR... 93

Chapter 10 PIMPING PAIN: THE IRONY OF COMMUNITY COMPASSION................. 106

Chapter 11 A BROTHER ON THE WAY...................... 111

Chapter 12 THE GOSPEL FOR THE GHETTO 121

Chapter 13 OVERCOMING VICTIMIZATION: *It Took all That!* 131

Chapter 14 SILENT CLERGY... 143

APPENDIX
    The Context – Richmond, California

    The Ministry – Bethlehem Missionary Baptist Church

FOREWORD

A Ministry that Saves Lives is written by a scholar-pastor who is equally at home in both the pulpit and the academy. In this manuscript, he writes with deep theological depth and broad sociological understanding using clear and non-technical language. His words are so very understandable until everyone who struggles with reading is able to identify with the description and the analysis of urban society, and the need for addressing societal ill with a carefully thought out theology. He has tested the ideas that he has written about and he offers both a theoretical and pragmatic to effective ministry. He communicates exceptionally well to lay readers using a sermonic style that shares personal experience. Hence, the book offers pleasure and profundity to the readers.

Very few thinkers can communicate with the clarity and compassion of Dr. Alvin C. Bernstine. If the reader would do repeat readings of the pages of this book, one will discover successive new meanings for urban ministry. I heartily recommend A Ministry that Saves Lives, not only for persons in urban ministry, but to all people of faith who are dedicated to either the possibility of, or the work of transforming society.

> Dr. J. Alfred Smith, Sr.
> Pastor Emeritus, Allen Temple Baptist Church
> Oakland, California

ACKNOWLEDGMENT

Special thanks to Adam Kruggel, a courageous organizer for Contra Costa Interfaith Supporting Community Organization, a PICO affiliate; Reverend Henry Washington, Operation Richmond, who daringly shares with me his heart, soul, and strength in doing prophetic ministry; the Ceasefire/Lifelines to Healing Working Group, who have the audacity to try something that has never been done before; Devone Boggan and the Office of Neighborhood Safety, who fearlessly take the ministry to the streets; to the Bethlehem Missionary Baptist Church that allows me the freedom to dream and the space to act; and the amazing octogenarian, Ruth Marshall, who weekly embodies the spirit of the ministry that saves lives.

A MINISTRY THAT SAVES LIVES:
Sermons and Thoughts on Ministry in a
Challenging Context

PREFACE

In 2006, I made a major life decision. I decided to return home. My decision might not sound like such a big deal, but factor in the fact that home for me represented the place of my birth, early childhood, adolescence, and early adulthood. Returning home meant coming back to the geographical and social setting of my formative years, youthful struggles, young adult folly, inclusive of initial sexual encounters and past criminal adventures (not that both are the same). Returning home meant returning to the places and spaces of my initial spiritual formation, as well as the initial community where I began the journey of Christian ministry. Returning home meant the potential of intensely reconnecting with people I remembered ; not all represented pleasant memories.

It had been 27 years since I had loaded up my meager belongings in a 1973 Chevrolet Monte Carlo, and began an academic journey at the once inimitable Bishop College, Dallas Texas, continuing to Vanderbilt Divinity School of Vanderbilt University, Nashville, Tennessee, and United Theological Seminary, Dayton, Ohio. My 27-year journey included ministry stops, beginning with my first assignment as Director of Christian Education at Westwood Baptist Church in Nashville, TN, to becoming the pastor of Olivet Baptist Church in Nashville and 13 years of serving as pastor of the renowned Mount Lebanon Baptist Church in Brooklyn, New York. Along the way, I had been favored to serve six years as Director of Family Ministry for the Sunday School Publishing Board, the publishing arm of the largest African American denomination in America, the National Baptist Convention, USA, Inc. This experience allowed me to form close associations with the convention hierarchy, personalities and convention dynamics. My life had been incredibly enriched and I believed that I was set to finish my ministerial journey at Mount Lebanon, and then I received "the call" to return home and serve as pastor of the Bethlehem Missionary Baptist Church in Richmond, California. Bethlehem represented the "home" church of my migrant father's spiritual pilgrimage and the place where he began his preaching ministry journey. He actually preached his first sermon and was licensed to preach on my first birthday.

Once again, I was loading up a car and beginning a cross-country trek, this time from Brooklyn, New York back to Richmond, California. Somewhere during that 3000-mile journey, I began to muse over the prospects of my next ministry assignment. I assessed where I was going, what I was getting into, who I was and what I brought into the ministry context. I considered the ministry: a staunch traditional congregation comprised mostly of "seasoned" saints. I also considered the context of the ministry: Richmond, California, a city besieged with violence. It had been cited in USA Today as one of the most violent cities in the country. I further considered what gifts and learning experiences I brought to the ministry and the context. It came to me that the assignment before me was to shape a ministry that saves lives.

Upon arriving at the Bethlehem Missionary Baptist Church in Richmond , I began forging the groundwork of shaping a ministry that saves lives. I began by preaching a series of sermons about the relevance, rationale, and reasoning surrounding such a ministry emphasis. To highlight my commitment to the ministry approach, we developed the church logo to include the phrase, "A Ministry that Saves Lives". Our logo has been included in everything that Bethlehem has presented, from programs, letterhead, flyers, impact cards, our website, to the church sign. As a congregation, we have provided ministry opportunities to address an array of social challenges that threaten black and Latino life. One of the featured works of Bethlehem Missionary Baptist Church has been the H.E.A.L. (Help Educate and Liberate) Conference, a collaborative with the Contra Costa Community College. In the H.E.A.L. Conference, we provide practical tools to strengthen family life and relevant interventions for psychological and emotional freedom.

In our work with community organizations, we partnered with Contra Costa Interfaith Supporting Community Organization, C.C.I.S.CO. A powerful alliance emerged where we worked in collaboration with the Latino community to confront our distinct and common communal challenges. With C.C.I.S.C.O., we established a powerful voice to address the challenges of the city, experienced significant victories, and garnered the respect and attention of the powers-that-be. We have hosted major community actions where a number of significant community-transforming initiatives launched. In response to a deadly shooting that took place inside one of the city's churches, we collaborated with Organization Richmond.

In 2010, we spent an entire year in serious study and reflection on how we could be the best church that we could be, within the world that we lived. Our theme was "B.E.G.I.N. Again in 2010". A Vision Team was formed and provided invaluable input on how to connect people with the pastoral vision. In summary, we began steering a traditional congregation toward a specific way of shaping the ministry, in response to the challenging context in which the church was set.

In 2011, something amazing began to take shape. I was invited to participate in the Ceasefire/Lifelines to Healing Initiative as a part of Contra Costa Interfaith Supporting Community Organization (CCISCO). Ceasefire/Lifelines to Healing is an anti-violence initiative in which community stakeholders collaborate with law enforcement to aggressively address potential perpetrators of violence. The Ceasefire approach has a track record of significantly reducing urban violence. Currently, Bethlehem Missionary Baptist Church has provided consistent and committed participation in the Ceasefire/Lifelines to Healing initiative. Our congregation has produced and presented some of the most engaged people, in an effort to eradicate the violence in the city of Richmond. We have a long way to go, but I am excited about the progress and prospects of the Ceasefire/Lifelines to Healing initiative, as well as the many other wonderful things that Bethlehem Missionary Baptist Church is doing in an effort to shape a ministry that saves lives.

The experience has become so incredible that I want to provide a sermonic recapitulation of how a traditional urban church began shaping a ministry within a challenging context, a ministry that saves lives. I admit that this publication may well represent my own personal need to revisit the biblical impetus of the journey. Yet, I hope that the following sermonic attempts will add to the work of shaping relevant ministry within the challenging context of urban America.

Along with the sermons, I include editorial opinions that I submitted to the local newspapers and African American weeklies. I also want to invite you, the reader(s), to interact. Thus, I have provided reflection questions to invite you to consider the issues that are shared in the sermons. I consider the reflections as an opportunity for congregations to become more thoughtfully engaged in community transformation. It is my hope that your reflections would serve to deepen your engagement as you minister within your particular contexts. If anything worthwhile emerges out of this publication, it will be because you consider these sermonic struggles worthy enough to ponder how we minister within communities that are besieged by violence.

Chapter 1

"APPRECIATING THE VALUE OF BLACK LIFE:
A Community Response to the Senseless Killing in the Black Community"

*by Reverend Dr. Alvin C. Bernstine,
Pastor of Bethlehem Missionary Baptist Church
in Richmond, California*

NOTE: The following is the unedited version of an article that I submitted for publication in Richmond Post, The Globe, and Sunday Morning News in 2008. These publications represent the weekly news provided to and by the African American community. This article provides a prophetic perspective for the ministry that has been shaped by the Bethlehem Missionary Baptist Church.

Presently, within communities inhabited by large constituents of African Americans, an alarming number of senseless killings take place. It has become common for once quiet and stable communities to be traumatized by the tragic killing of young black men, many of whom once had such promise and potential. As a result, yellow crime scene tape, marking off areas with bloody bodies draped in canvas, has become a symbol of communities seemingly left for dead. Many of us are faced with the disturbing distinction of living in cities that are characterized as "the most dangerous cities in America."

Richmond, California is one of those cities. For the last five years, Richmond has consistently been listed in the top 15 most dangerous cities in America. Richmond has joined Detroit, Newark, Camden, and Oakland as constants among those of such ignoble distinction. The common criteria for being considered a dangerous city is to possess a considerable African American community - characterized by African American youths who are locked in pockets of poverty - communal despair accentuated by generational self-hatred, and the availability of drugs and guns.

Richmond has engaged in a number of symbolic responses to the senseless killings in the street, such as Tent City, community marches, and the recent "Ring the City with Prayer" effort. It has been noted that during these symbolic activities, the killings decrease. Yet, as soon as the tents are removed, the marchers go home, the prayers stop – the killings return.

> *It has become common for once quiet and stable communities to be traumatized by the tragic killing of young black men, many of whom once had such promise and potential.*

The question that lingers is: what are we going to do to stop the senseless killings within the black community? Any careful analysis of the communities in which the killings take place will reveal an acute need for strengthening the family structure within the black community; a need for social policies that are sensitive to a community plagued with a history of neglect and exploitation; a living wage that allows for adequate family support; and a shaping of communally generated values that counteract the demonic values of the dominant culture, where anything is acceptable as long as it makes money.

Although the above responses require formidable strategizing and committed engagement, there is a response to the senseless killings within our communities that is within our immediate reach. This response is for each of us within the African American community to participate in appreciating the value of black life. We express our appreciation of black life when we acknowledge that the life of each person is valuable enough for us to protect, even at the risk of our own. This does not mean that we start jumping in front of guns. It basically means that we see black life as being so sacred that when one life within the community is not safe, then no life within the community is safe.

> *We express our appreciation of black life when we acknowledge that the life of each person is valuable enough for us to protect, even at the risk of our own.*

What has fueled the escalating rise of killings within our communities is the loss of value for black life. This loss of value is expressed when, every time there is a killing within the black community, black people inevitably respond by stating that no one saw anything and no one knows why the person was killed. Unless it is a person of wealth, stature or fame, such as a Chauncey Bailey or Sean Taylor, we claim to have not seen anything and have no clue as to why someone's son is now lying dead in the streets.

I was raised in the black community and one thing I discovered is that someone is always looking at what everyone else is doing, and someone always knows something about what other people are doing. The nosiest people I know are black people!

The same must be true of other communities because no one is getting away with senseless killings within other communities. The only difference is that people in other communities value life to the extent that they'll tell what they see and they'll let others know what they know. Blacks, however, have collectively decided that the lives of young black men have no value and aren't worth anyone telling what he or she knows. Our ominous silence has literally fueled the escalating violence within our communities, because a few killers believe that it's okay to kill blacks and no one is going to say anything. If we really want to stop the violence – let's stop the silence!

I am not advocating snitching! I am advocating caring! We must care enough for the lives of our people that we refuse to allow a few people to desecrate the sanctity of life in fear of our own lives. We know the names and faces of those who are responsible for most of the killing in Richmond, as well as the motives for the killing. If we value life to the extent that we no longer want to see bloody bodies draped in cloth, and yellow tape signaling our collective depreciation for life, we must send a message of intolerance for people who indeed lack an appreciation for life. It is a risk that we must take, but it is a risk worth taking. If we choose not to take this risk, then our city remains numbered as a dangerous place to live, and since no one cares, it makes it a good place to die. If we stop the silence, we stop the violence! Let us love black life enough to make murder too expensive for the perpetrators of violence, as they face the high cost of increased community isolation and inevitable prison incarceration.

> *If we stop the silence, we stop the violence!*

REFLECTIONS

1. What social realities do you think have contributed to the devaluation of black life?

2. How do we move from symbolic responses to substantive responses when it comes to the violence within our communities?

3. Create a context where a discussion can take place about the relationship between community silence and community violence.

Chapter 2

A MINISTRY THAT SAVES LIVES:
"Stepping Up"

TEXT: "But at midnight Paul and Silas were praying and singing hymns to God, and the prisoners were listening to them. Suddenly there was a great earthquake, so that the foundations of the prison were shaken; and immediately all the doors were opened and everyone's chains were loosed. And the keeper of the prison, awakening from sleep and seeing the prison doors open, supposing the prisoners had fled, drew his sword and was about to kill himself. But Paul called out with a loud voice, saying, ' Do yourself no harm, for we are all here.' Then he called for a light, ran in, and fell on down trembling before Paul and Silas. And he brought them out and said, 'Sirs, what must I do to be saved?' So they said, 'Believe on the Lord Jesus Christ, and you will be saved, you and your household.' Then they spoke the

word of the Lord to him and to all who were in his house. And he took them the same hour of the night and washed their stripes. And immediately he and all his family were baptized. Now when he had brought them into his house, he set food before them; and he rejoiced, having believed in God with all his household. " (Acts 16:25-34, NKJV)

Today's sermon actually summarizes the vision of ministry that God has appointed the Bethlehem Missionary Baptist Church. We are at a critical juncture in history where God wants us to get serious about the seriousness of the gospel, which is literally saving lives. Jesus said, "I came to seek and to save that which is lost." All around us, lives are being lost, and we are being called to shape a ministry that saves lives.

When the church sees itself as being in the business of saving lives, a sense of urgency emerges which dispenses with any activity that trifles and interferes with our mission. When we see ourselves as being responsible for saving lives, then our level of creativity intensifies to the point where we really believe that "with God all things are possible." We will try whatever is necessary and money is not an issue when saving lives is our reason for existence. When we know that we are here for the purpose of saving lives, an attitude shift takes place where we "know that we are more than conquerors in Christ Jesus." The resurrection lives when we really believe that God has appointed us as life-savers because "the sting is taking out of death and the grave is robbed of its victory."

I am clear on what my role is: I am responsible for sharing with you what God is calling for at this present time. I am also clear on what your role is: You are responsible for heeding God's call and sharing the task with me to shape a ministry that saves lives. For us to really make a difference, we must get past trying to be cute, proper, fly, all of that and some. God is calling for a church that will shape a ministry that saves lives.

This vision of ministry was further confirmed as I listened to the guest preachers of the Progressive Missionary Baptist District Association: Drs. Fred Campbell and Joseph Ratliff. Dr. Ratliff noted that we spend too much time and energy trying to impress and not enough energy trying to make an impact. I want to announce from the start that my tenure as pastor will not focus on being impressive, but on being impactful. Being impressive has its place, but being impressive does not save lives. To save lives, we must do as Paul and Silas did: harness our energies and resources to make an impact.

Maybe a review of the Devil's mission statement could shock us into realizing the seriousness of our ministry. Jesus said that the Devil's mission is to steal, kill, and destroy. The Devil is busy taking what does not belong to him, killing all whom he did not give life, and destroying all that has been created to give God glory.

The story of Paul and Silas' journey into the Philippian jail provides powerful insights into shaping an impactful ministry that saves lives. Paul and Silas were brought together because God needed a team who could work together. Paul split with Barnabas and John Mark because the

> *Being impressive has its place, but being impressive does not save lives. To save lives, we must do as Paul and Silas did: harness our energies and resources to make an impact.*

ministry that God needed in Philippi needed a different team. Barnabas and John Mark continued to work for the Lord, but they worked in Cyprus. God teamed up Paul and Silas for the work in Philippi.

We can make too big of a deal over the fact that certain people don't work well together. The truth is: certain people don't work well together! We forget that the work is more important than personalities. Moreover, God has always found a way to get people to do His work, even if God has to break up some leadership teams to get His work done. God teamed up Paul and Silas to do a specific job, at a specific time, at a specific place. God has brought us together for a specific job at this specific time, and at this specific place.

The ministry in Philippi started off well. They had "good church" down by the riverside. They had good fellowship with good church folk. They were blessed with a warm reception at Lydia's house. There were no critical issues to confront, no destructive drama to disarm. After several days of good fellowship, however, an annoying personality emerged. An enslaved young girl kept showing up, bothering the preacher, and consequently, disrupting the ministry. The Bible notes that she was bright and gifted, but she was enslaved and was being used to advance the prosperity of others. She kept showing up, annoying the preacher and disturbing the fellowship. Every time the church would meet, she would show up. Like some people I've met in church, she believed that her anointing called her to annoy the preacher and disturb the fellowship. After several days, Paul got sick of it. She provoked Paul to speak in the name of Jesus and he commanded the devil to take flight. The Bible says, "And he came out that very hour."

A ministry that saves lives has to sometimes exorcise anointed annoyances. Paul shows us that there is only so much that preachers and church folks need to take from annoying personalities. After awhile, we must step up and command devilish annoyances to take flight. Please do as the Bible has shown : acknowledge that he or she has gifts, not necessarily bad or evil, but enslaved by an evil spirit. People are not always bad or evil, but enslaved by a spirit that allows them to be exploited and made a fool of.

Bethlehem has a noble history, and I know much of it. We started off well. I can remember many good times we had here, good fellowship with good church folk. Yet, it never ceases to amaze me how good church folk tolerate annoyances. Church folk need to know that the devil knows that we are nice, good, and don't like to make trouble. Yet, there comes a time when even good church folk must step up to annoying personalities and speak boldly in the name of Jesus. When annoying personalities are allowed to irritate the preacher and disturb the fellowship, we are blocked from the ministry that God has purposed in our lives. We need to know that when we step up to annoying personalities, we literally become agents of that person's salvation.

> *When annoying personalities are allowed to irritate the preacher and disturb the fellowship, we are blocked from the ministry that God has purposed in our lives.*

I have seen God do too much in my life to allow the ministry that God is working through me to be sabotaged by annoying personalities. I love everybody, because I know that God loves everybody. However, I also know that if people have hell in them, then I have to love the hell out of them. We must love people enough to step up and confront them when an annoying spirit is trying to destroy their lives.

Please note, however, there was money attached to the annoying personalities. The young girl was worth money to those who enslaved and exploited her. And wherever money is the issue, other demons will surely raise their heads.

What Bethlehem needs to know is that any and every threat to life in our communities is being motivated by money. As annoying as some of the personalities in our communities can be - with their loud music, crazy clothes, bad talk, high crime, and senseless violence – there is money attached to the madness. There are people getting rich off of our people's crazy annoyances. As annoying as some of the behavior can be, there is money attached to the madness. As annoying as the constant threat of terrorists, wars and rumors of wars, can be, there is money attached to the madness. If we don't believe that there is money attached to it, then start commanding some of these devils to take flight and watch who comes knocking at your door. Even in the church, all annoying personalities usually have an ungodly interest in the money.

Paul and Silas got in trouble because they dared to step up to the annoyances against the ministry. A ministry that saves lives has to get fed up to the point where we step up to the annoyances. Jesse Jackson told us the other day, "It's not enough to be right, if we have no fight. We win not because we are right, but because we fight." Joe Ratliff noted that we sing all of these Christian songs about fight, and have all of the biblical imagery of being in a fight, but no one is fighting. Civil rights were not won because we were right. We won because we stood up and dared to fight.

Paul and Silas got sick of the annoyance and decided to step up and fight. As a result, they were whipped and thrown in jail. However, in the darkest hour of their painful plight, they sang and prayed to God. As the sores on their backs lay open from the wounds of the whip, they sang and prayed. Heavy shackles weighted their legs and limited their movement, but they stepped out of their own pain and stepped up into praise and prayer.

> *Stepping out of our own pain and stepping up into praise and prayer makes God attractive.*

What amazes me the most about this text is that it states, "And the prisoners heard them." Those who shared in their bondage listened to the words of their freedom. Although they shared a common cell, something about the response of Paul and Silas moved the prisoners to want to hear them. The prisoners saw the pain and gore of Paul and Silas's situation, but they listened to them. Paul and Silas made praising God so attractive that others wanted to hear. Stepping out of our own pain and stepping up into praise and prayer makes God attractive.

Listening implies an interest that leads to understanding. Who's listening to us? A ministry that saves lives has something to say that catches the attention of those whose lives are at risk. We must get creative enough to make praying and praise attractive to people whose lives are at risk. This is no time to be cute and proper. Praise and prayer ought to fit the situation, and not be reduced to empty rituals.

I don't know about you, but I wouldn't be here today if someone had not stepped up and made God attractive enough for me to want to hear. Beginning with the late Reverend C. R. Hamilton, a long list of people stepped up and made prayer and praise attractive enough for me to hear. I heard people speak out about their own pain. I heard people give praise in the midst of problems. I heard people be real with God and tell God exactly what was going on and how they felt. I have even heard people curse in their prayers as they lay their souls bare to God. They were not cursing God, but cursing that which brought them to God. People who get real about their own issues, problems, pains, difficulties, failures, and weaknesses can provide a ministry that saves lives.

The Bible says, "Suddenly there was a great earthquake, so that the foundations of the prison were shaken, and immediately doors were opened and everyone's chains were loosed." I have lived outside of California for the last twenty-seven years. Half of my life has been spent in other parts of the country. People from other areas of the country commonly express paranoia of earthquakes. Also, a well-known observation about church life in California is a need for an earthquake. Christians, all around the country, see where church life in California needs to be shaken up. Christians are too laid back, too blasé, too "at ease" in California. God needs to shake up the California Christian community.

The truth is: whenever God's people get real about ministry, something is going to happen. Whenever God's people step up and get serious about being a witness for the Lord, something will happen. Let God's people step up and we will witness God shake some stuff up. Let us step up and get real about prayer and get serious about praise, and we will see some things getting shook up around here. Some of the cultural foundations and political realities that are hindering our people will be shaken, and some new doors will open, and the chains that have been hindering us will be loosed.

Someone came here today bound and bloody, and the church needs to provide a witness that can save that life. Someone here needs a door opened in order to save his life. Is there anyone here willing to step up and be used by God? Someone here needs shackles to be loosed, so that she can be free in God.

Maybe that's what happened to the songwriter when he sang:

Jesus saved my soul in the middle of the night.
I got so excited and I didn't try to hide it.
Jesus saved my soul in the middle of the night.

REFLECTIONS

1. What are the life-threatening issues within your community?

2. Does your church/organization's work revolve around the above-mentioned life-threatening issues? If not, why?

3. What are your thoughts on stepping up to annoying personalities?

4. Create a discussion where the entities that profit from keeping your community stagnant can be identified.

Chapter 3

A MINISTRY THAT SAVES LIVES:
"Speaking Up"

TEXT: "But at midnight Paul and Silas were praying and singing hymns to God, and the prisoners were listening to them. Suddenly there was a great earthquake, so that the foundations of the prison were shaken; and immediately all the doors were opened and everyone's chains were loosed. And the keeper of the prison, awakening from sleep and seeing the prison doors open, supposing the prisoners had fled, drew his sword and was about to kill himself. But Paul called out with a loud voice, saying, 'Do yourself no harm, for we are all here.' Then he called for a light, ran in, and fell on down trembling before Paul and Silas. And he brought them out and said, 'Sirs, what must I do to be saved?' So they said, 'Believe on the Lord Jesus Christ, and you will be saved, you and your household.' Then they spoke the word of the Lord to him and to all who were in his house. And he took them the same hour of the night and washed their stripes. And immediately he and all his family were baptized. Now when he had brought them into his house, he set food before them; and he rejoiced, having believed in God with all his household." (Acts 16:25-34, NKJV)

> Never before in history has so many people lived in so many life-threatening contexts.

Again, I offer to you what I strongly believe to be the primary vision that God has assigned this ministry, if not the ministry of the African American church nationwide. I pray that all who share in the ministry to the people in the "hood" would understand that we are at a critical juncture in history, where God is calling for us to get serious about the gospel and to literally save lives. We are being summoned to participate in Christ-centered ministry that seeks to save that which is lost. God is looking to each one of us to do whatever it is we do in order to shape a ministry that saves lives.

Never before in history has so many people lived in so many life-threatening contexts. We are at a place in history where we can give incredible witness on how the power of God saves lives. We are the people that God is seeking to use as instruments of life in a world filled with the mechanics of death. In a time in which morticians are more profitable, better staffed, and more technologically advanced than most churches, we are being called upon to save lives. Churches open for two hours on Sundays and one hour for choir rehearsal on Thursdays, while mortuaries are open 24/7. Yes, you and I, as members of the Lord's church, are being called upon to be the difference between life and death for so many of our Bay Area brothers and sisters. What we do in the next few years will literally stop some young people, black men and women, from doing what the Philippian jailer wanted to do: kill themselves. I don't know about you, but I am excited because I know that God has placed me on a mission to save lives.

May I say again: we are not here to major in impressing other church folks. We are here to make a life-saving impact. As a pastor, I am not here to do everything I can to make people like me. I learned from Jesus that people who love you are going to love you anyhow, and people who are not going to love you are not going to love you no matter what you do. I've known love in my life and I have discovered it to be true: when people love you, you can't do any wrong, and people who don't love you are busying themselves looking for what's wrong with you. Also, I am not trying to gain any "brownie" points, because no one can do more for me than what God has already done. I just want to be a part of what I know is a God-movement, and right now, God is moving us, positioning us to shape a ministry that saves lives.

Consider again our text. We learned from Paul and Silas that a ministry that saves lives goes through changes in leadership, because some people just don't work well together. Paul and Silas came together because Paul and Barnabas could no longer work together. We also noted that a ministry that saves lives has to step up to annoying personalities. We have to step up to people who engage in behavior that annoys the preacher

A MINISTRY THAT SAVES LIVES

and disturbs the fellowship. After several days of annoyance, Paul stepped up to the annoying behavior of a young woman who was being exploited for monetary gain. Please don't forget that money can usually be found at the root of all annoying behavior. Also, money-motivated behavior can be life threatening. People will hurt you over money, as well as tear up the Lord's church over money issues.

Paul and Silas landed in jail because they dared to step up to an annoying personality. While in jail, they stepped out of their own pain and stepped up into the presence of God through praises and prayer. A ministry that saves lives is attractive because it gets the attention of those who don't normally hear anything good about God, nor see church people in an attractive light.

While in jail, an earthquake shook the jail to its very foundations. The doors of the prison swung wide open, and the chains and shackles of the imprisoned fell to the ground. The mean jailer, who had cruelly locked Paul and Silas in maximum security, feared that all the prisoners had escaped. The escape of the prisoners would have signaled to the powers-that-be that the jailer had failed in his responsibilities. The fear of failure overwhelmed the jailer to the point where, rather than suffer public humiliation and death, he would rather kill himself. Paul spoke from the deadly ruins of the situation and said, "Do yourself no harm because we are all here." I hear, echoing from the dungeon of Paul's experience, powerful insights that speak to us in this hour. I hear some words that are tailor-made for people in the urban ministry on how to shape a ministry that saves lives.

> *The church shapes a ministry that saves lives when we can speak from the witness of we-ness.*

The first word that gives shape to a life-saving ministry is "we". Paul understood that the primary fear of the jailer was that some prisoners had escaped and that he, alone, would suffer the consequences. Paul spoke up and his words informed the jailer that there was no need for him to follow through with his self-infliction intentions, because everyone who was supposed to be there was there. The church shapes a ministry that saves lives when we can speak from the witness of we-ness. In a world where people suffer from the fear of aloneness, we save lives when everybody who is supposed to be here is here, and is where he or she is supposed to be.

Just before Ray Charles died, he completed two wonderful projects. He completed his life story for the big screen, for which Jamie Foxx won an academy award. He also completed a comprehensive collection of songs that he had collaborated on with other recording stars, entitled "Genius Loves Company". Jesus organized the church in such a way that it best operates when we see ourselves as connected. Read the Book of Acts, and from Chapter 16 to the conclusion, note how the narrative shifts from individuals to "we". "We" is so important to the church's ministry that it is stated ninety-seven times in the final eleven chapters of Acts. Paul is so committed to the we-ness of the church that when he further elaborated on Christian truths, he said: "We are more than conquerors." "We know that all things work together for the good to those who love the Lord and are called according to His purpose." "We have this ministry in earthen vessels."

Someone needs to hear me, today, because what pushes people to the brink of self-infliction is the painful sense of being abandoned, disconnected, isolated, and left alone to deal with life's crises. People need to know that the church of the Lord Jesus Christ is the one place where you can tap into the we-ness of life. "We are all here!" Some church folks need to hear me as well, because nothing destroys a church's witness more than when the we-ness shifts to me-ness. What God wants to do with the church is not about "me", nor is it about "you", but it's about "we"! To all who believe, the church is about you; you need to make a note that the defining truth about the Bible is that there is but one God, and He is not me or you.

What really stirs up the we-ness juices is when we consider that everyone who was in jail was an alleged offender. All of them had been accused of something, and all had come to the jail from different forms of offense. Can I speak up? If the Bible holds true, all who make up the church are offenders. We are not alleged offenders. We are not suspected offenders. We are guilty offenders, because the Bible says, "All have sinned and come short of the glory of God." Therefore, let not one of us think too highly of ourselves because our best dress is like filthy rags before God.

I need to leave this point, but when I think about my own journey, no one person deserves all the credit. God used a lot of people to affect my salvation. Even now, my life is blessed because God has put me in touch with the we-ness of life. No

> We give a great testimony when our stories have some collective blood on them.

one alone can completely affect God's salvation. A ministry that saves lives operates from a sense of we-ness that liberates people from the death-inflicting aloneness of me-ness.

The earth shook. Foundations were shaken. Rubble and debris had fallen heavily upon the prisoners. Within a paranoid and oppressive government, the personal charges, or offenses of most of them, were serious enough for the death sentence. The fear of death was certainly heightened by the shaking of the earthquake. It was clear that all who were in prison were in a crisis, both personal and communal. In a normal moment, all should have fled and sought to save himself. Yet, Paul's words to the crisis-stricken jailer indicated that all the prisoners stuck together during the crisis. All of the prisoners were on the scene, all marked present.

A ministry that saves lives can speak up when there is a powerful sense of "here-ness". We can speak up when we are on the scene, when we are where we are supposed to be. Brothers and sisters, we are called to stick together in the midst of crisis, both personal and communal. We give powerful witness when other crisis-bound people see us sticking together during crises. Our ministry is most authentic when we live through certain challenging events. We give a great testimony when our stories have some collective blood on them.

I was living in New York during 9/11. I ministered to people through 9/11. I buried and memorialized people whose bodies were never recovered. However, the one thing I remember most about 9/11 was how New Yorkers came together during the crisis. New York is known for its dog-eat-dog pace, every-person-for-himself mentality. However, 9/11 showed the world how a crisis can make New Yorkers come together.

Every day, people are having their own personal and private 9/11's. The enemy is terrorizing our homes, schools, neighborhoods, and even our churches. Richmond has been classified as the eleventh most dangerous city in the country, which I believe is quite astounding. California schools are considered hopeless. Oakland is on the brink of breaking a new murder record. One church has planted a garden of crosses for every homicide committed in Oakland this year. What this community needs is a witness of here-ness. The needs of Richmond and Oakland speak to the terrorized of our communities, informing people that we are here!

"We are all here!" That's the testimony of a ministry that saves lives. We are here in the crisis. We are here in the midst of the terror and pain. We are not running off. We are not tucking our tails and fleeing from the scene. We are not locked up behind the safety of our stained-glass windows. We are not leaving the city. We are here in our schools, here on our streets, here in the neighborhood. We are here, taking back our communities. We are here, sticking together, even while the earth quakes and the foundations shake. "We are all here!"

It should also be noted that Paul was in a position to see the jailer about to kill himself. He could speak because he was in a position to see the life-threatening realities of the jail and the jailer. A ministry that saves lives has to be in a position to see clearly. In order to speak up, we have to have an authentic perspective. What we do in the community, and in the sanctuary, has to mean something in the lives of the people with whom we live.

The text that defines ministry for me is John 1:14, "And the word became flesh and dwelt among us." Jesus positioned Himself to see so that He might save. He saw that the harvest was plenteous, but the laborers were few. He saw that people were scattered as sheep without a shepherd. He saw human hurt. He was in a position to see the pain. He did not hide in religion, nor take sanctuary in holiness. In fact, He despised the superficiality of a religion that made no difference in the lives of people. For us to be a ministry that saves lives, we have to be in a position to see, so that we too can give an authentic cry, "Do yourself no harm, for we are all here."

I am somewhat embarrassed by my final observation in this message. I'm embarrassed by what it reveals to me about how we have been conditioned to worship and praise God. The Bible clearly notes that while in jail, within a crisis situation, in an unfriendly environment, among hostile authorities, Paul and Silas were praying and singing. It appears that Paul and Silas were having better church in jail than many of us have in church. Their worship of God was so powerful that the work of Christ was manifest.

> I'm embarrassed, my brothers and sisters, because so much of what we do in the name of God is not relevant.

It seems that what empowered Paul and Silas to perform a ministry that saves lives was a relevant sense of God-ness. It did not matter to Paul and Silas where they were, be it in the synagogue, the riverside or the jailhouse. The relevancy of God makes the work of God real in a difficult situation.

I'm embarrassed, my brothers and sisters, because so much of what we do in the name of God is not relevant. In fact, we have become quite adept at worshiping God within contexts of irrelevance. Worship is not relevant where the work of Christ is not manifest. Christian worship is supposed to make the work of Christ so real that someone comes running, asking, "What must I do to be saved?" For a ministry to save lives, we must make worshipping God so relevant that Christ becomes real in desperate situations.

There is a verse in one of our favorite hymns that warrants our attention. In the hymn, "Must Jesus Bear the Cross Alone", there is a verse which says:

To serve the present age, my calling to fulfill;

May all my powers engage to do the Master's will.

My best witness ought to be my worship, and in my worship, Christ ought to be so relevant that someone is moved from the darkness of despair and asks, "What must I do to be saved?" Wherever you give God your best worship, someone ought to be moved to ask, "What must I do to be saved?" No matter the situation, be it good or bad, let's give God our best worship, because there's always someone on the brink who needs to come forth, asking, "What must I do to be saved?" Even if we have to do like Paul and Silas, expose our wounds and speak from the places of our pain; I believe that bleeding wounds for God are always relevant. Let's worship God with fresh wounds and someone will see the work of Christ in our lives. When desperate people see that God is real in our worship, they will ask, "What must I do to be saved?" HALLELU-JAH! PRAISE HIS NAME!

REFLECTION

1. Where does your community rank among the state, region, or nation, in terms of violence?

2. In what ways is your church speaking up, or addressing the violence within your community?

3. How are the churches within your community "positioned" to provide an authentic witness to the at-risk African American youths?

4. Create a context where your congregation, or community leaders, can address ways to be better present with the desperate and at-risk within the community.

Chapter 4

A MINISTRY THAT SAVES LIVES:
"Giving Up"

TEXT: "But at midnight Paul and Silas were praying and singing hymns to God, and the prisoners were listening to them. Suddenly there was a great earthquake, so that the foundations of the prison were shaken; and immediately all the doors were opened and everyone's chains were loosed. And the keeper of the prison, awakening from sleep and seeing the prison doors open, supposing the prisoners had fled, drew his sword and was about to kill himself. But Paul called out with a loud voice, saying, 'Do yourself no harm, for we are all here.' Then he called for a light, ran in, and fell on down trembling before Paul and Silas. And he brought them out and said, 'Sirs, what must I do to be saved?' So they said, 'Believe on the Lord Jesus Christ, and you will be saved, you and your household.' Then they spoke the word of the Lord to him and to all who were in his house. And he took them the same hour of the night and washed

their stripes. And immediately he and all his family were baptized. Now when he had brought them into his house, he set food before them; and he rejoiced, having believed in God with all his household." (Acts 16:25-34, NKJV)

I want to lift up again what I believe, more and more, to be the primary vision that God has to shape the ministry of those of us who serve in urban America. More than ever before, I am convinced that the continued relevance of the church depends upon us getting serious about the seriousness of the gospel, which is to literally save lives. We can no longer trivialize what Jesus prioritized; that is to "seek and to save that which is lost." All of the many great and wonderful things that God has done for us as individuals, and as a church, have been set-up material for what God wants us to do in this hour. God is expecting us to respond in faith toward the shaping of a ministry that saves lives.

I don't know that you saw as you journeyed through the week, but everywhere I looked, I saw lives at risk. I saw men and women, boys and girls, in positions of desperation, where all it would take is a shake of their fragile worlds, and like the jailer in our text, they would seek to kill themselves. Some of you looking at me are also living lives so fragile that all it would take is a mere shaking of your world and you would push some button of desperation. All it would take is a shake-up of your job, a shake-up of your family or your marriage, a shake-up of the economy, or a shake-up of your health. Clearly, this is no time to be cute. This is no time to style and profile, and no one needs to strut and stroll. It's time to take God seriously and shape a ministry that saves lives.

As we further pondered over our text, a powerful truth emerged that literally has the power to save our lives. You probably said, "Brother Pastor, my life is not at risk." In a physical sense, you are probably right. However, when we honestly consider our walk with God and our life in Christ, then most of the church folk I know are living spiritually risky lives. As far as doing what God wants us to do, most of us are living lives that need to be saved from the slow death of mediocrity. Most of us do just enough to suggest Christianity, or some socially accepted form of religiosity.

> *As far as doing what God wants us to do, most of us are living lives that need to be saved from the slow death of mediocrity.*

The pacifist Quaker, Parker Palmer, has some words that speak powerfully to us now when he was forced to ask himself, "Is the life I'm living the life God wants to live in me?" God showed me something in this text that has the power to save us from not living the life that God wants to live in us. If we take Acts 1:8 seriously, as the spiritual table of contents of the book of Acts, then we see what's happening in the lives of Paul and Silas as being totally initiated and orchestrated by God. Everything that happened to Paul and Silas, including the plight of the jailer, was being initiated and orchestrated by God. What transpired throughout this narrative was being directed by God.

I shared with you last in the precious message that what pushed Paul and Silas to sing and pray - to offer worship and praise, while suffering in a jail - was a powerful sense of God-ness. A powerful and relentless sense of God-ness shaped the drama of our text. Read Acts 16 and note that the only reason Paul and Silas were in Philippi was because God had set up a detour from their desired destination and commissioned them to go there. They initially sought to go to Bythinia, but God summoned them to Macedonia. They were where they were because of God. God's call to Philippi led them to the riverside church; placed them in the hearts of the Lydia; put them in the path of an annoying personality; got them in trouble with the powers-that-be; had them stripped of their clothes and whipped on their backs; and God landed them in jail.

I know some brothers who have served time and were saved, and they all tell me that God had placed them in jail to save their lives. Their ministry saved the young woman's life from exploitation and manipulation. Paul and Silas went through all they went through because God wanted to position them in a place to save lives. God placed them there, and we all know that it was God who sent the earthquake, that shook the foundations, knocked the doors off the hinges, loosed the chains, and broke the shackles. It was God who moved so mightily that rather than run and have a compromised freedom, being wanted fugitives always looking over their shoulders - all the prisoners stayed in place.

God put the jailer in a predicament of desperation, where his only thoughts were to kill himself. However, God also had Paul and Silas in a position to step up and speak up, so that the jailer would give up his insane plan to kill himself.

We have to believe that the drama of our lives has godly meaning, and that God has used the often strange, confusing, even painful episodes in our lives to position us to be instruments of salvation. Whatever may be going on in our lives right now, a powerful sense of God can enable us to realize the ministry that God has called us to. We are being placed in a position to step up, speak up, and give up, because "all things work together for the good for those who love the Lord and are the called according to his purpose."

> *Maybe the church needs to repent of wasting opportunities to save lives, because we thought what was going on needed to be voiced in complaints.*

Maybe the church needs to repent of wasting opportunities to save lives, because we thought what was going on needed to be voiced in complaints. Maybe the church needs to seek forgiveness and a renewal of the Spirit, because we confused eternal victories with temporary defeats. Maybe the church needs to spend time in sack cloths and ashes, mourning over some of the stupid meetings we've held, the crazy opinions we've expressed, talking about nothing, while people were dying in sin. I know, in my own life, I have misinterpreted the drama in my life as my drama, when in fact it was God's drama to put me in a position to save lives. Everything I have experienced, gone through, and survived had been arranged by God to give me a relevant ministry to save lives. I confess that I have had some powerful opportunities to step up, but I stepped back. I've had some opportunities to speak up, but I held my peace. I've had opportunities to give up, but I gave in. Praises be to God, for God has been merciful to allow you and I another opportunity to recommit to a ministry that saves lives.

The jailer sought to kill himself, but "Paul called with a loud voice, saying, 'Do yourself no harm, for we are all here.'" A word should be said about the fact that Paul spoke loudly. He spoke with enough force to get the jailer's attention. Could it be that the volume on our words of salvation has been too low to get people's attention? Paul's words were forceful enough to get the jailer's attention, and the jailer's response provides us with insights on a ministry that saves lives. The jailer's response was to give up.

The first thing that the jailer gave up was his sense of social superiority. In verse 24, we noted the jailer taking his job so seriously that he pushed the envelope and intensified the pain of Paul and Silas. He locked them in maximum security and fastened their feet in stocks. He thought his position in life was so important that he would oppress other people to secure it. In verse 27, he feared that his position in life had been shattered and the people he oppressed had fled. He feared that his position was lost, so rather than be socially executed, he went to kill himself.

Paul's words to him moved him to reconsider his position and seek another position. In verse 29, "He called for a light, ran in, and fell down trembling before Paul and Silas." Mind you, all the other prisoners saw him as well. They saw the big, bad jailer trembling on his knees and pleading to prisoners for his life. He did not care who saw him, because he took being saved seriously. He knew that his life as an oppressor of people, of ruling over people, was over, and for him to live, he needed to get down and be with the very people he once oppressed.

All around the country, the churches that are experiencing new life are those that give up any sense of social superiority. The bourgeois, wanna-be-upper-middle class, perpetrating church is dying a horrible death. Churches that are making a difference in the world are those that come off their high horses, lower their snobby noses, and get down to where the people are. We have to give up any notions of being better than other people. Give up wanting to be bigger than others. Give up wanting to be so smart, so right, so holy, so classy, and literally being so out-of-touch. Whatever is keeping us from being down with the people, we have to give it up.

God had some witnesses in the jailer's life who, when he came down, could be used to save his life. The jailer humbled himself and asked, "Sirs, what must I do to be saved?" The same jailer who had intensified the pain and oppression of Paul and Silas humbled himself and gave up all notions of self-security. All that he thought he had going on to secure himself was lost. He wanted to be saved, but he knew that he could not save himself. He needed salvation, so he asked, "What must I do to be saved?"

A ministry that saves lives must give up any and every notion of self-security. One of the great sins, if not the greatest sin of today's church, is the crazy belief of some to save the church. There are people in the church, today, who foolishly think that they have a responsibility to save the church. Churches are in courts all around the country because some misguided, unbiblical, non-spiritual folk believe that they have been anointed to save the church. Where in the Bible has God asked anyone to save the church?

God said, "The gates of hell shall not prevail against it." In other words, any Satanic force, including misguided church folk, will never sustain a victory against the Lord's church. A ministry that saves lives has to give up any and every notion of self-security, and seek the salvation of the Lord. Our salvation is not within ourselves, but it is in the giving up of ourselves. Give up pride! Give up self-importance! Give up inflated egos! Give up any and every belief that we can save ourselves with anything about ourselves!

Paul and Silas joined in unison and said, "'Believe on the Lord Jesus Christ, and you will be saved, you and your household.' Then they spoke the word of the Lord to him and to all who were in his house." The Bible says, "And he took them the same hour of the night and washed their stripes. And immediately he and all his family were baptized." When the church gave him the answer to his plight, he was then nurtured in the Word. His response was to minister to those whom he knew were in pain. He engaged in a healing ministry and his whole family was baptized.

A ministry that saves lives gives up any hindrances that prevent a healing ministry. My Brooklyn pastor, Dr. Johnny Ray Youngblood, has aptly stated, "All ministry is healing and ministry that is not healing is not ministry." Some of us need to accept the fact that all who are members of the church are not without personal pain. All of us are hurting somewhere from something. However, we have too much stuff in the way that prevents people from engaging in a healing ministry within the church, let alone a healing ministry outside the church. What we cannot do well inside the church, we will never do well outside the

> *What we cannot do well inside the church, we will never do well outside the church.*

church. We have too much stuff in the way.

For one, we make being Christian too difficult. We complicate what God has simplified. The jailer asked, "What must I do to be saved?" They said, "Believe on the Lord Jesus Christ, and you will be saved, you and your household." We have added too much other stuff. We say, "Believe and act like us. Believe and do like us. Believe and dress like us. Believe and talk like us. Believe and sing like us. Believe and be cheap like us. Believe and worship like us."

We also make too many other things more important than the Bible. Constitutions, by-laws, positions, dues, meeting, eating and greeting have become more important than the Bible. Our text tells us that they "spoke the word of the Lord to him and to all who were in his house." He was nurtured in the Word. People who engage in a healing ministry are empowered by the Word.

I don't know about you, but I want to be healed. I want to be made whole. I don't want to bleed to death, but in order for that to take place, we have to give up what hinders us from a healing ministry. Jesus didn't let anything prevent Him from the healing ministry. He healed on the wrong day, at the wrong place, and at the wrong time. He gave up the Sabbath! He gave up the Law! He gave up traditions! He gave up constitutionality! He even gave up Himself to save all who were lost.

Bethlehem needs some Jesus folks, who will give up pointless protocol! Give up rigorous rituals! Give up tired traditions! Give up constitutional correctness! Give up loaded legalism! Give up the need to be right! Give up the need to win! Give up yourselves so that healing can take place.

The Bible keeps speaking to us. It tells us that the jailer brought them home, fed them, "and he rejoiced, having believed in God with all his household." Finally, a ministry that saves lives needs to give up joyful praise unto God. There needs to be a greater witness of God in our midst. Such a witness comes when we give up joyful praise unto God.

I am often concerned for those who seem to sit up front, but have less joy. It looks like the closer to the front some people get, the less joy they have. Too many church leaders act as if they have never had a sense of God in their lives. Maybe you are not ready to give up a joyful praise, but I know that God has been real in my life. I was like the jailer, positioned to kill myself, not with a sword or gun, but with self-destructive living. But one day, God positioned some Christians to get my attention and let me know that I didn't have to kill myself. God saved my life. He saved me from drugs. He saved me from gang-bangers. He saved me from ignorance. He saved me from kryptonite friends and killer enemies. He saved me from myself!

So every opportunity I get, I give up joyful praise. I give up thanksgiving. I give up a hallelujah! I give up a joyful shout! I know that everything that has happened in my life, is happening, and will happen, God wants me to use to save lives. HALLELUJAH! PRAISE HIS NAME! GIVE IT UP! GIVE IT UP!

REFLECTION

1. Identify moments when your church, or the congregations within the community, repented of being out-of-touch with the painful realities within the community.
2. Can you name some status claims that your church needs to consider giving up, in order to become more effective in its ministry to the community?

3. What will hinder your church from giving up issues that are clearly in the way of it becoming a force for community transformation?

4. Create a context among the leaders of your church where personal and communal worship can be assessed as an authentic experience for the work of Christ.

Chapter 5

HELPING YOUR HOMETOWN:
Ministry with a Focus

TEXT: **"The Spirit of the Lord is upon Me, because He has anointed Me to preach the gospel to the poor; He has sent Me to heal the brokenhearted, to proclaim liberty to the captives and recovery of sight to the blind, to set at liberty those who are oppressed; to proclaim the acceptable year of the Lord." (Luke 4:18-19, NKJV)**

The late, great thinker, inventor, mathematician, scientist, and scholar, Albert Einstein once said, "No problem is fixed with the same level of consciousness that created it." Einstein, who also wrote profusely on the issue of race and the oppression of African Americans, sought to teach us from the vast laboratory of lessons that he had learned. No problem is ever corrected with people thinking the same way they did when the problem

> *No problem is ever corrected with people thinking the same way they did when the problem was created.*

was created. We might appease ourselves with our well-phrased suggestions. We may even provide a temporary solution to a persistent situation, but in order for us to bring about lasting solutions to the issues that plague us, we must somehow be elevated to a new way of thinking.

The problem of violence in our city has brought us to the point where we must elevate to a new way of thinking. The thinking that has created the problem will not solve the problem. The politics that created the problem will not solve the problem. The economics that created the problem will not solve the problem. The laws that created the problem will not solve the problem. Nor will the religion or models of ministry that created the problem solve the problem. If we are to help our hometown, then there has to be a radical shift, a refocusing of our thoughts so that we might shape a ministry that saves lives.

> *If we are to help our hometown, we too must know that our foe is white supremacy and domination, but our focus must be on the most vulnerable in our society, who are being destroyed by the environment created by those who profit from it.*

As I pondered over today's assignment, I had some sense of what needed to be said, but I didn't know how to say it. After twenty-nine years of preaching ministry, I have learned that it is not always what you say, but how you say it that wins the day. I considered the issue of violence in our city to be so serious that I did not want to waste any moment to say what I believed needed to be said.

I have also learned that if I really wanted help in saying what needed to be said, then it was best to consult Jesus and see what He had to say. Jesus provides for us an incredible way of not only saying what needs to be said, but He also helps us to minister with focus. Focusing on the early days of Jesus' ministry provides a way for us to help our hometown. Our hometown will only be helped when we address the socio-spiritual evil that has produced an environment where violence provides African American men with a wrong means toward a right end.

The young men within our community are reacting to, or acting out of, a social environment that is being upheld and maintained by a spiritual evil. Paul was correct when he said, "We fight not against flesh and blood, but against principalities, against powers, against rulers of the darkness of this world, against spiritual hosts of wickedness in high places." Yet, Paul also knew, as did Jesus, that the foes of our fight were manifest in society and causes wholesale destruction upon the most vulnerable in the society. Jesus saw it in His time, and we better see it in our time that our fight is with the foe, but our focus should be on those who are the most vulnerable to the evil of our foe.

The old preachers used to tell us that if you really want to understand a text, study what comes before and what comes after it. What comes before our text is Jesus' experience in the wilderness where He is tempted by the Devil. The Temptations of Jesus center around three things: economics (bread), political exploitation (kingdoms of this world), and manipulative religion (using God for self-glory). What comes after our text is

Jesus struggling to authenticate His ministry, so that He might begin His ministry with the casting out of unclean spirits.

Our text represents the announcement of Jesus' ministry, which uses a text in Isaiah that focuses upon the most vulnerable in an oppressive society. Jesus informed the people of His hometown that His anointing was to focus upon the poor, those who were economically vulnerable; the brokenhearted, those who were psychologically and emotionally vulnerable; the captives, those who were socially vulnerable because of social restrictions; the blind, those who had no clue as to what was happening to them; and the catch-all, the oppressed, those who were vulnerable to the decisions and policies set by those who benefited from keeping society as it was.

Just as the Babylon experience wreaked havoc on vulnerable people, Jesus saw where the Roman experience was wreaking havoc upon vulnerable people. Jesus knew who the foe was, but His focus was upon those who were being destroyed by the environment of the foe. Just as Isaiah knew that Babylonian oppression was the foe, Jesus knew that Roman oppression was the foe. Just as Isaiah focused his ministry upon those who were being destroyed by the oppressive environment of the foe, so did Jesus. If we are to help our hometown, we too must know that our foe is white supremacy and domination, but our focus must be on the most vulnerable in our society, who are being destroyed by the environment created by those who profit from it.

In one of my many learning experiences on undoing racism, a white sociologist noted that unless we seek to understand white supremacy, everything else we try to understand will only serve to confuse us. When I listen to the people of my hometown discuss the escalating violence in our community, which has made Richmond the eleventh most dangerous city in America, it sounds as if we are totally confused. We point to unemployment, lack of adequate education and job skills, broken homes, fatherlessness, drug addictions and trafficking, learning disabilities, lack of government commitment, and so on, as reasons for the violence. Yet, all of the above social maladies are the results of an environment created by white supremacy and white domination. Our young men are products of an unhealthy environment that makes them vulnerable to violent reactions and actions.

If we are confused with the questions to our problem, then we are more confused with the solutions to our problem. I say, "Shame on us who think that more police, more jails, harsher prison sentences, containment of the black community, just say no to drugs, war on poverty, or a war on drugs will curtail or prevent the violence in our communities." I used to train dogs to attack. The fastest and easiest way to train a dog to attack is to aggravate it, annoy it, or tease it . I had some friends who fed their dogs gunpowder or hot food. Adding more police to the black community, and more jails and harsher sentences, is annoying; it aggravates, because black folk know that the only reason we have police is to protect white people and white people's property.

I am not saying that law enforcement is not necessary in the black community, but historically, police have never been good news for black men. Tent cities, marches, and sleep-outs are fine, but the reality is that they are only temporary and sometimes symbolic gestures that offer no long-term solutions. I believe that to help our hometown, we must do like Jesus -

focus our ministry. We must not fool ourselves regarding who is the foe. Our sons and brothers are not the foe, nor are white people. When we speak of white supremacy and white domination, we do not refer to a people. We refer to the systems and structures that inform our society, whereby certain people, by virtue of skin color, have privileges that come at the expense of oppressing others. White supremacy and white domination represent a way of thinking, a social consciousness that gives some access to privilege and denies others those same privileges.

> *White supremacy and white domination represent a way of thinking, a social consciousness that gives some access to privilege and denies others those same privileges.*

There is a foe, but our focus is on those who are most vulnerable within the environment created by the enemy. Jesus said, "My ministry in my hometown will give good news to the poor. I will tell people who are being denied access to economic privilege that 'the earth is the Lord's and the fullness thereof, and all who dwell therein.' I will tell the poor that the good news for poor people is the hope that poverty is not eternal. In fact, 'Blessed are the poor in spirit, for theirs is the kingdom of God.'"

Jesus said, "To those who have been emotionally and spiritually injured within this sick environment, healing is possible. You who have been emotionally broken and spiritually splintered, there is a Balm in Gilead. Likewise to those who have been bound by the evil forces of an oppressive environment, I want to focus on you and proclaim liberty for your bondage. The truth about identifying who the real foe is, and the focus upon the most vulnerable, is a liberating truth that frees brother from self-destruction." Jesus said, "The truth shall make you free."

Jesus also said, "To all who are being oppressed within this inhuman, artificial, godless, and Satanic environment, you, too, shall be free. African Americans will be free from the violence of oppression, and white Americans will be free from the lies of being the oppressor." Jesus concludes His message by saying, "To proclaim the acceptable year of the Lord." In other words, the time to do God's bidding is now. The time to help the hometown is now. The time to shift our thinking, and to quit trying to fix our home with the same thinking that messed it up, is now. The time to get involved and focus on the most vulnerable is now!

Must Jesus bear the Cross alone,
And all the world go free?
No! There is a cross for everyone.
And there is a Cross for me.

REFLECTION

1. What are your thoughts on Einstein's observation, "No problem is fixed with the same level of consciousness that created it"?

2. Do you see in your church and/or community where problems are being addressed with the same level of consciousness that created it? Where?

3. How does your church discuss the subject of white supremacy?

4. Create a context where a discussion can take place among church leaders regarding the focus of Jesus' ministry and today's church.

Chapter 6
"MAKES ME WANNA HOLLER"

TEXT: "Hanani one of my brethren came with men from Judah; and I asked them concerning the Jews who escaped, who had survived the captivity, and concerning Jerusalem. And they said to me, 'The survivors who are left from the captivity in the province are there in great distress and reproach. The wall of Jerusalem is also broken down, and its gates are burned with fire.' So it was, when I heard these words, that I sat down and wept, and mourned for many days; I was fasting and praying before the God of heaven. And I said: 'I pray Lord God of heaven O great and awesome God, You who keep your covenant and mercy with those who love You and observe Your commandments, please let Your ear be attentive and Your eyes open, that You may hear the prayer of Your servant which I pray before You now, day and night, for the children of Israel Your servants, and confess the sins of the children of Israel which we have sinned against You. Both my father's house and I have sinned. We have acted very corruptly against You, and have not kept the commandments, the statutes, nor ordinances which You commanded Your servant Moses. Remember, I pray, the word that You commanded Your servant Moses, saying, "If you are unfaithful, I will scatter you among the nations, but if you return to Me, and keep My commandments and do them, though some of you were cast out to the farthest part of the heavens, yet I will gather them from there, and bring them to the place which I have chosen as a dwelling for My name." Now these are Your servants and Your people, whom You have redeemed by Your great power, and by your strong hand. O Lord, I pray, please let Your ear be attentive to the prayer of Your servant, and to the prayer of Your servants who desire to fear Your name; and let Your servant prosper this day, I pray, and grant him mercy in the sight of this man' For I was the king's cupbearer." (Nehemiah 1:2-11 (2-4), NKJV)

One of the most powerful and inviting expressions of the Christian faith is expressed in the psalm, "Make a joyful noise unto the Lord." The psalmist invites us into joyous noise-making, literally hollering in response to the awesome goodness of God. We generally have no problem getting people to respond to the goodness of God. Most of us have evidence in our lives where God has blessed us, healed us, delivered us, made a way for us, set us free, and saved us. I know at BMBC, on any given Sunday, we have no problem inviting people to wanna holler in response to the wondrous works of God.

Our relationship with God serves as the foundation, so that no matter what's going on in our lives, we are confident that God is up to something. When I read the story of our text, however, I am challenged by the fact that if my relationship with God is authentic, real, and genuine, then I should have the capacity to feel some of what God feels. My relationship with God should provide me with some sense of how God feels about what's happening in the world and the condition of His people. In other words, our relationship with God should not only invite us into shouts of joy, but make us wanna holler over the conditions within our community. Moreover, the church's potential for meaningful ministry is predicated upon us having the capacity to feel the pain of our broken and wounded communities. We have to feel it before we can heal it.

When the late crooner, sexual-healing practitioner, Marvin Gaye, made a prophetic shift in his songs, with the production of Inner City Blues, he included in that multi-platinum cut a song entitled, "Makes Me Wanna Holler." Marvin Gaye looked with the eyes of a prophet upon the broken and wounded conditions of urban America and sang, "It makes me wanna holler, and throw up both my hands." When he saw how monies were being spent on meaningless governmental projects, while poverty raged in the streets, he sang, "It makes you wanna holler and throw up both your hands." When he experienced the rising inflation and economic depression that crushed people who were unable to pay their taxes, he sang, "It makes me wanna holler and throw up both my hands." As he gazed upon the increasing violence, the social hang-ups and personal bad breaks, "It makes me wanna holler and throw up both my hands."

Nehemiah got the news of how terrible distress, great grief and painful shame were plaguing his people, and it made him wanna holler. From the safety of a good civil service job, which offered him privilege and security, he could still feel the pains of a wounded and broken community and it made him wanna holler. The Bible says, when he heard about it, he was knocked off his feet and bent in tears, and for many days, he was sunk in grief. At the time of his most painful reaction, he didn't even see what was going on. He just heard about it. He hadn't been in the neighborhood for some time, but just hearing of the devastation, the despair, distress, and shame-based condition, moved him to holler. Before he even went and saw it for himself, just hearing about it made him wanna holler.

I sometimes wonder if we have lost the capacity to deeply feel the pain of our broken and wounded community. As people of God, people called by His name, have we so counterfeited our relationship with God that it does not matter if we feel what God feels, as long as we have access to our places of privilege and security? As long as God is blessing us, as individuals, or as a congregation, it appears that we are not always interested in feeling what God feels, because it might cause us to identify with the broken and wounded. We don't want to feel it because it might make us wanna holler and throw up both our hands.

If we feel the pains of the homeless, shame-based, drug-induced, violence-prone, despair-filled people whom we pass on our way to our places of privilege and security, it might make us wanna holler. If we feel the pain of the young sisters who have been forced into sexual slavery, or the young brothers who see no future beyond the narrow confines of ghetto economics, it can literally make us wanna holler and throw up both our hands. If we feel the pain of those in distressed neighborhoods, conclaves of urban violence and despair, it can make us wanna holler and throw up both our hands.

Our lack of capacity to feel the pain of our broken and wounded world prevents us from engaging in transformational ministry, so we reduce the world-changing power of God to pageantries of privilege and security. Our pageantries of privilege and security are often our gaudy anniversaries, Women in White, Brothers in Blue; the Ushers have an Annual Day, and so the Choir does, too.

Not so with Nehemiah! Even from a position of privilege and security, he felt the pain of a wounded and broken community - a community traumatized by broken walls and burned gates. He did not go to church and make a joyful noise, or lift up his hands in praise. Nor did he just holler and throw up his hands in disgust or despair. He hollered to the Lord. The Bible says that he prayed before the God of heaven.

Nehemiah allows us to see that experiencing the pain of our broken and wounded, shame-bound communities should move us to see that what's going on is a God thing. The ruins of the walls were symbolic of the loss of a sense of God's protective presence. The text indicates that some escaped, but others survived. Those who survived had lost a sense of God's protective presence.

Some of us remember a song that was once popular in our churches, "Lord, be a fence around me day by day. Lord, protect me as I travel along the way." The pain of Nehemiah's community resulted from losing a sense of God's protective presence. What do people do when their community has lost a sense of God's protective presence? How do the survivors make it when there is no sense that God is with you?

Since leaving Richmond, I have developed an academic ecclesiology, an understanding of the church. Yet, my hometown understanding of the church is the one that shapes me. Whatever else my understanding of church is, it always believes that the church, or the people of God, symbolizes the protective presence of God. Something has happened in our communities when the church becomes the last place for the broken and wounded. I get the calls all the time, "Reverend, I have nowhere else to turn, so I turn to the church." People try everything else, and then the church! Nehemiah went to God in prayer because he understood that what was making him wanna holler was a God thing.

Maybe that's why people don't gather in prayer. Prayer has a way of making us feel what God feels. Maybe prayer has become too painful for the church of privilege and security, because prayer will make us wanna holler. Prayer will remove us from our self-obsessions toward being God-possessed, and that causes us to feel what God feels.

While in prayer, Nehemiah also allows us to see that experiencing the pain of a broken and wounded community moves us to see that what's going on is a sin thing. The burning of the gates was a symbol of the people having lost access to a prosperous future. There was no way to get to God's blessing

> *The consequence of sin is always a loss of access to God's prosperous future.*

because of the ravages of sin. The consequence of sin is always a loss of access to God's prosperous future.

Nehemiah prayed to God and included in his prayer the acknowledgment and confession of sin. What made Nehemiah wanna holler was the painful realization that the brokenness within his community was the result of God's people not living up to the standards of God. "All had sinned and missed the mark." The people were missing the mark of accessing God's blessings, because they were not being faithful to the things of God.

Although Babylonian oppression was a harsh aspect of the people's plight, Nehemiah could in no way put full blame on the white folks. The people had so internalized their oppression that they were acting like the oppressor and oppressing one another. He said, "Both my father's house and I have sinned." It ought to wanna make us holler when we not only have lost a sense of the protective presence of God, but we have also lost a sense of sin. We limit sin to sex stuff when, in fact, sin is anything that deprives us from the riches of a wholesome relationship with God. Whatever is keeping you from having full access to a wholesome relationship with God, that's sin; that's a burning gate.

No one walks through a burning gate, because it's a symbol of sin and shame. Can I pull the church in here? Whatever else the church represented, it once symbolized the reality of sin. The reason we had churches was because people outside of the church needed to be saved from sin, and the sinners in the church needed help with sin. The church was not only a symbol of the presence of God, but also a symbol of the presence of sin. Where there is a loss of a sense of sin, it makes me wanna holler.

Nehemiah also allows us to see that experiencing the pain of a broken and wounded community moves us to see that it's a redemption thing. The walls were broken down - no sense of the protective presence of God. The gates burned - no sense of the reality of sin. It made him wanna holler, but not throw up his hands. Nehemiah wanted God to put something in his hands. Nehemiah put it on God, "Now these are Your servants and Your people, whom You have redeemed by Your great power, and by Your strong hand…Let your servant prosper this day."

> *Nehemiah helps us to see that success and prosperity are doing the will of God in a way that helps the broken and wounded of the community.*

Here is where the prosperity gospel falls short. Success and prosperity are more than personal privilege and security. Nehemiah helps us to see that success and prosperity are doing the will of God in a way that helps the broken and wounded of the community. Where people have lost a sense of God's protective presence, and have no sense of sin, that's a redemption thing. That is a time when restoration, revival, and renewal are to be the order of the day.

When Jesus looked upon the harvest, He saw a waiting harvest. He saw sheep without shepherds, broken and wounded. He saw wearied and scattered flocks, folk in despair, with no access to a prosperous future. He said, "The harvest truly is plentiful, but the laborers are few. Therefore, pray the Lord of the harvest to send out laborers into His harvest."

It made Jesus wanna holler, but not throw up His hands. It made Him holler and God put something in His hand. For the cause of redemption, nails were put in His hands. For the cause of freedom, nails were driven into His feet. For the cause of justice, a sword was pierced into His side. For the cause of salvation, a rugged cross He bore. He didn't throw up His hands; He threw out His hands for me and for you. He gave us a sense of God in our midst, for He was called, "Emmanuel, God with us." He gave us a sense of our sin, for He "came to save His people from their sin." Yet, He also gave us a future, a glorious future, "That at the name of Jesus every knee shall bow… and every tongue shall confess, that He is Lord, to the glory of God the Father". HALLELUJAH! PRAISE HIS NAME!

REFLECTION

1. How are you personally, economically, and socially situated in relation to the people in your church's community?

2. What is your understanding of sin? The church? Redemption?

3. Can you identify any issues in your community that could make you "wanna holler and throw up both your hands"? List.

4. Create a context in which you and the leaders of your church and/or organization can identify issues where you can reach out your hands in love.

Chapter 7
THE POLITICS OF KILLING STREETS

NOTE: The following represents another opinion that the editorial board offered to the local African American newspapers. This was a response to a bewildering chain of events following a fist-fight between contentious elements of African American young men. The fight took place within the office of a City Hall-based entity, the Office of Neighborhood Safety. The ONS is a city agency that is designed for one purpose alone: addressing the gun violence within the city of Richmond. A fist-fight that never escalated into gun violence became political fodder for shameless activity between politicians, community leaders, media, and law enforcement.

On urban streets across America, young African American men, ages 18-25, are killing one another over ghetto politics. Ghetto politics consist of turf protection, which is killing over land that none of them own; rooster complexes, killing for young women who will eventually leave them for another man; urban respect, killings over perceived looks of disrespect, which were really looks of fear; and retaliation, which are killings based upon misunderstandings around any of the above. Ultimately, the politics of killing streets result from young men having to create identities from the collective ruins of failed social systems.

> *Every social system - including family, church, school, and judicial system - has failed to protect these young men from the brutal realities of the killing streets.*

Every social system - including family, church, school, and judicial system - has failed to protect these young men from the brutal realities of the killing streets. In a very real sense, African American young men who are most at risk are victims of failed social systems.

In my home town of Richmond, California, where I currently serve as a pastor of a local congregation, the politics of killing streets have expanded. They have expanded into the petty and personal squabbles of community leaders, who are fighting over the best solution to ending the violence. The politics of killing streets include political leaders publicly vowing to destroy and dismantle the one organization that is providing evidence-based results in reaching and relating to the young men who are most involved in the killings. The Richmond Office of Neighborhood Safety has championed the cause of eradicating the violence on our streets. The Office of Neighborhood Safety employs Neighborhood Change Agents, who connect with at-risk young men, many known shooters, in the very ways that society has failed them. They befriend, mentor, and relate to these young men in some of the most amazing ways, creating opportunities for personal and communal transformation.

Yet, our city has witnessed the petty antics of a city councilman, who has a personal vendetta against the director of ONS and commits scarce city resources to the dismantling of this effective agency. The politics of killing include law enforcement and self-promoting community leaders who are unable to build authentic trust so that a collaborative Ceasefire/Lifelines to Healing initiative can radically reduce the killings in Richmond; instead, they promote the tragic process of warehousing young African American men in prisons. Law enforcement's obstinate commitment to doing business-as-usual inhibits effective community policing, and community-based organizations are being led by people who are more concerned about being in charge than making a difference.

The politics of killing has the media running weeks-long series over fist fights, confusing editorial comments, and the sensationalizing of whatever it finds newsworthy. The politics of killing even include ego-deficient clergy who are unwilling to work together, and others who are unwilling to participate in a community-driven initiative because of bewildering racial views. The politics of killing have morphed into political and community theatrics, which have become quite amusing, even to the young men who potentially kill.

I recall a rather powerful perspective on politics provided by soon-to-become United States Ambassador and legendary civil rights leader, Andrew Young. While campaigning for Jimmy Carter, Andrew Young met with Richmond clergy. I was a very young preacher and was invited to come along and share a luncheon with him and the Richmond clergy. I listened and watched as he gently and wisely provided a clergy-friendly definition of politics. He said that politics was about making sure you got a piece of the pie. As we watch the politics of killing being played out in Richmond, it might be time for Richmond citizens to find out who is getting the biggest slice of the pie from the killings. Is it a political payoff for the blind politician, self-promoting community organizers, law enforcement? Or is it simply good news for a reporter who happens to be in bed with the blind politician?

REFLECTIONS

1. Can you identify a time in your community when a community crisis was politicized?

2. What are your thoughts about the relationship between law enforcement and the African American community?

3. Create a context where your congregation and/or community organization can identify the ones who benefit from maintaining the status quo in your community.

Chapter 8
THE MINISTRY OF COFFIN STOPPING

TEXT: "Now it happened, the day after, that He went into a city called Nain; and many of His disciples went with Him, and a large crowd. And when He came near the gate of the city, behold, a dead man was being carried out, the only son of his mother; and she was a widow. And a large crowd from the city was with her. When the Lord saw her, He had compassion on her and said to her, 'Do not weep.' Then He came and touched the open coffin, and those who carried him stood still. And He said, 'Young man, I say to you arise.' So he who was dead sat up and began to speak. And He presented him to his mother" (Luke 7:11-17, NKJV).

I don't believe that I have shared with you my life-long desire to be one of Jesus' disciples. I know that He has a lot of disciples, but I want to be one in the number. I want to be one of those persons whose life and living is being daily shaped by the teachings and ministry of Jesus Christ. I want to be one of those who walk by faith and serves in obedience to the One whom I believe has the liberating message of the kingdom.

As uncertain as a disciple's moments are, being a disciple is a privilege. As a disciple, I get ring-side seats to see the Master work the miraculous majesty of His ministry. As a disciple, I get to see God at work in the complex affairs of twisted and damaged humanity. As a disciple, I can even experience the joy of witnessing blind folks receiving sight, lost folk becoming found, crippled folk getting a leg up on life, weak folk getting strength, deaf folk hearing, rejected folk being received, and I even get to see dead folks coming alive.

In my 30-plus years of being a disciple, I've been blessed to have my own failures forgiven, my faults ignored, my weaknesses understood, and to be lovingly picked up when I fell down. Yet, in all of my days of being a disciple of Jesus, nothing challenges me more than the ministry of coffin stopping. Becoming a consistently decent preacher has been a monumental task for me! I was actually content with being a choir member, usher, and even took a futile shot at being a deacon. I never wanted anything to do with being a pastor, but the Lord had other plans. I've taught, organized, administrated, raised money, served in the community, wrote books, and even spent some time trying to provide sanity to the insanity of the National Baptist Convention, USA, Inc. Yet, nothing seems to be as daunting a task as the ministry of coffin stopping.

By the way, all of us have been invited into the ministry of coffin stopping. Whatever else we have been doing as a disciple of Jesus, you too must join with the disciples who followed Jesus to Nain, where we are given a live demonstration of what it means to be in the ministry of coffin stopping. In a nutshell, the ministry of coffin stopping is to intentionally interrupt the systemic processions that are prematurely putting our young men in graves. The ministry of coffin stopping exists for the purpose of bringing to a halt the painful processions that carry the tragic cargo of premature deaths. The ministry of coffin stopping engages the ministry of Jesus in bringing life into places and processes that are known for death. In the words of my dear friend, Reverend Elliot Cuff, we blackmail death to reclaim the black male. We fulfill the objectives of the ministry of coffin stopping by obediently adhering to the calling of Jesus Christ.

For those of you who don't want to be a part of this ministry, the text has a place for you. You are assigned to the crowd, and if you like numbers, it is noted as a large crowd. Yet, you will not be identified as a disciple of Jesus. For the text says, "That he went into a city called Nain; and many of His disciples went with him, and a large crowd." If you claim to be a disciple, however, your refusal to stop coffins not only assures the constant flow of young men to early graves, but it is a blatant act of disobedience against the call of Christ. Jesus leads disciples into the ministry of coffin stopping.

I suspect that some texts we struggle to hear, but in Richmond, where young black lives are in a constant procession into early graves, we ought to clearly see the message of this text. In Richmond, where, in one week, 8 young men died in homicides, we ought to clearly hear this text. However, forgive me for not assuming biblical clarity among the congregation and allow me the pastoral privilege of providing lenses through which we might better see and hear this text. The text states that Jesus went into a city called Nain, accompanied by His disciples, and the aforementioned large crowd. "And when He got near the gate of the city, behold, (or look what I see!), a dead man was being carried out, the only son of his mother; and she was a widow. And a large crowd was with her."

The city of Nain, which means 'pleasant', was located 25 miles from Capernaum, within view of Mount Hermon. In a city where the name means 'pleasant', everything that Jesus saw coming from the city was not pleasant. He saw a dead man being carried out. He saw a funeral procession. He saw a weeping, broken mother, and He noted that she was a widow and the boy was her only son. Accompanying her was a large crowd, many of them professional mourners. They lived for a good funeral. Their work was to facilitate healthy grief and they loved their job.

The text does not tell us how the young man died, nor did Jesus ask, like many of us, "What happened to him?" The Bible says, "When the Lord saw her, He had compassion on her and said to her, "Do not weep." For us to understand and appreciate the focus of Jesus' ministry, it might be helpful if we knew that, within the Jewish community, a son signified a future. As a widow, a woman with a dead husband, an only son was an economic safety net. As painful as the premature loss of a husband is, a widow could see her way to a future as long as she had a son. With a son, there was always hope for the future, as well as her economic well-being. Without a son, her family had no future, and she was doomed to the ravages of poverty. She would be left to live off the arbitrary whims of her community.

What Richmond needs to see is that there is value in black life. The only people who don't seem to know the value of young black men are the black men taking black life. There is so much value in black life that California spends $267,000 a year to serve one black youth in California Youth Authority, and less than $10,000 a year for education in a public school. There are some people in this state who live well off of the pathological forays of black life. Bethlehem needs to understand that without functioning, capable, competent young black men, we have no future. We need to revisit our Judeo-Christian roots and reshape our perspective on the value of boys and young black men. Boys guarantee us a future! The ministry of stopping coffins is a ministry of the future!

"When the Lord saw her," a vulnerable member of the community whose future was at risk, "He had compassion." I hold that any ministry that makes a difference is energized, motivated, and created by people with compassion. Folk without compassion can't see human suffering. All they see is to just have a church, hold programs, and perpetuate insignificant auxiliaries. Jesus had compassion on a community whose fu-

> *There is so much value in black life that California spends $267,000 a year to serve one black youth in California Youth Authority, and less than $10,000 a year for education in a public school.*

ture was at risk and He did something about it. The Bible says, "Then He came and touched the open coffin, and those who carried the boy stood still."

I need to park here for a moment because something of tremendous importance is being dramatized. According to the laws of the Jewish community, to touch the dead was to be labeled unclean and declared unclean for 7 days. As a member of the unclean society, one would not be allowed to participate in the activities of the community, including religious rites and rituals. Jesus knew that, but to stop a coffin that bore the future of a community, He risked being declared unclean! He risked being excommunicated from the community in order to restore someone to the community. He risked being isolated so that someone can be restated.

> The ministry of stopping coffins is a ministry to the unclean.

The ministry of stopping coffins is a ministry to the unclean. We will never stop the endless processions of premature deaths if all we are willing to touch is that which is clean. These young boys and girls may appear unclean with their saggin' pants, bling-bling, broken English, ghetto slang, and tarnished families, but they are our future. In three years, I can count on one hand the number of young brothers who have graduated and gone to college at BMBC, yet many are being left untouched because we consider them unclean. If they are unclean, then the ministry of stopping coffins is to clean them up!

Notice, also, that those who were carrying the brother stopped when Jesus touched the coffin. He stopped those who had been designated to take the young man out of the community and bury him. Just as the coffin represents a structure designed to carry the dead, there are institutions, systems, and policies that are designed to take us out. I know of no black-owned gun manufacturer in the world. Yet, someone is manufacturing, supplying, and giving our young boys access to weapons of destruction and that needs to stop. The politics of indifference upheld by apathetic politicians need to be stopped. If the police in Nashville can trace one gun sold by one man to one woman who happens to kill a black celebrity, then surely they can trace the ones who are selling all these guns in Richmond. All of the systems, institutions, and policies that devalue black life need to be touched by the ministry of coffin stopping. If we just got out of these walls and showed up at some places, we would be surprised at the stuff that stops from a communal touch. What we are trying to do with the ONS (Office of Neighborhood Safety) is to touch some stuff, some of which is being held by the powers at the gate. There are gate-keepers in Richmond, people who sit in power, that we need to stop and we can stop them with a touch of communal power and conviction.

I have more text than I have sermon, and you will give me time, but Jesus does three other things. The first is to speak resurrection speech. He said, "Young man, I say to you, arise." He speaks to the dead with authority and power, and commands the young man to rise.

I shall always hold dear to my heart Mrs. Barbara Bankston, former professor and division leader of Laney College. As a bewildered young man, dead in cultural craziness, she spoke resurrection speech into my life. While out near the swimming pool, smoking weed, hanging out, trying to be cool, she stepped

> We can't be scared of the dead stuff surrounding our young men.

up to me and declared, "Alvin, you can do better than this." I was in two of her classes and she had been noticing my work, watching me being content with being average, uncaring, doing just enough to get by. All I wanted was the BEOG to finance my dead lifestyle. Yet, she stepped up to my weak, stinking self, and spoke resurrection speech that set a fire in me; I got up from there and have been trying to do better ever since.

We can't be scared of the dead stuff surrounding our young men. Like me, maybe they are not listening to Momma or Big Momma, and Daddy is absent. They may need to hear another voice. They may need to hear from someone who sees nothing good coming out of good families. For us to sit around and talk about them, rather than talk to them, does nothing but assist death. Let's use what we have best – a resurrection speech. If we are going to stop coffins, then we are going to have to step into the faces of our death-bound young men and women and declare: "Young folk, I say to you arise." "Get out of that slouch, pull your pants up. Girl, pull your skirt down, and get out of this coffin."

The Bible says, "So he who was dead sat up and began to speak." The young man's actions have moved me into a deep period of repentance for some of my treasured assumptions about what it means to be a man and what is best for boys. The young man is released to speak. In William Pollack's monumental work, Real Boys, he cites that some of the beliefs we hold about what's best for boys actually destroy boys. By shame and separation, we traumatize boys into wearing masks that disguise who they are and what they actually feel.

As a boy, I can testify to being told that boys don't cry, to hide my pain, don't show emotions, man-up, tough it out, be cool; it was the worst thing that ever happened to me. As boys, we are made to put on masks to hide pain, disguise true feelings, uphold an image, put on a front, and basically be what we're not truly feeling. I've hurt my own sons with the sickness, by discouraging how they need to feel about whatever they are feeling. Is it any wonder that boys fail, suffer from ADD, and have learning difficulties? How can boys learn, achieve, and be real, when they are all confused about how they need to be feeling? Could it be that the rage our boys are expressing, in the senseless destruction of one another, is the pipe-bursting of generations of stuffed feelings? It just might be that our self-hatred is being perpetrated because we hate feeling like we feel, so it's easy to kill someone who you know feels like he's dead anyhow.

> *It just might be that our self-hatred is being perpetrated because we hate feeling like we feel, so it's easy to kill someone who you know feels like he's dead anyhow.*

If we are going to stop the coffins, then we are going to have to provide opportunities for young people to be released to speak. Quit telling young people to shut-up! Quit telling them how they need to feel, what they need to say, and how they need to say it. Let them feel what they need to feel, and let them speak. If they are talking crazy, then let them keep

> Separation is traumatic, and separation from mother is most traumatic.

talking until they hear their own craziness and start making sense. Some of you adults talk crazy now because you never had the opportunity to be released to speak. We can stop coffins if we help young people to find their voices without depending solely on Snoop Dog, Fifty Cent, Li'l Wayne, Keisha Cole, Little Kim, or Tupac Shakur. Moreover, if they ever really hear Jesus' voice, then they will soon start talking like Him.

Suffer me one more observation, because what Jesus does next absolutely demolishes some of our treasured assumptions about raising boys. As much as we struggle to critique social systems and policies that conspire to destroy us, we run from critiquing ourselves. However, the actions of Jesus shatter our uncritical assumptions about what is best for young men. Jesus gave the young man back to his mother.

Pollack argues that boys in America suffer the greatest trauma when they are separated from mothers much too soon. When we put a clock on when young men need to be separated from the one who has been the primary source of nurture, warmth, love, and acceptance, then we inflict trauma. It often starts in kindergarten, where young 5-year-old boys are left alone to tough it out. Separation is traumatic, and separation from mother is most traumatic.

What we have done in our families, our communities, and even the church is to label boys weak, sissies, uncool, and unfit, if they can't make it alone. As a result, we have produced a nation of men who are actually left-alone boys. Whatever else a prison does, it intensifies aloneness. Reentry is difficult for men who have been abused in aloneness. Yet, prison is the one place where men cry out from the pain of being alone.

If we are going to stop the coffins, then we are going to have to reconnect boys with their mothers and men with the community. A coffin-stopping ministry may call some of us left-alone brothers to testify how dead we feel when alone. We can even be married or have serious relationships, and yet still live life as if we are alone. Jesus gave the boy back to his mother, and He's trying to reconnect us to the community, to the places where it's alright to be vulnerable, weak, flawed, and needy.

The Bible says, "Then fear came upon all, and they glorified God, saying "A great prophet has risen up among us, and God has visited His people." We want to see some real praise in Richmond, BMBC, my house and your house. Stop a coffin! Let the world see young men getting up, young men speaking up, and young men reconnecting to their community, and those who are just being curious will have to give God praise.

We create praise moments when young men reconnect, recommit, and renew their primary relationships. We create praise moments when mothers have tears wiped from their eyes and joy restored in their hearts. We create praise moments when communities have brighter futures and young people live with hope. I can speak for myself: Jesus reconnected me to my mother, my community, the church, and myself. I have much to praise God for, because the Lord spoke resurrection into my dead life, gave me my voice, and reconnected me to my people. HALLELUJAH! PRAISE HIS NAME!

REFLECTIONS

1. What are your thoughts on the violent behavior being displayed by young African American men?

2. Can you identify any structures that currently facilitate the demise of African American men?

3. Are there people in your community that you are afraid to touch? Name them.

4. Create a context where your congregation and/or organization can discuss the faulty parental assumptions being perpetrated by African American families to the detriment of our boys.

Chapter 9
A MINISTRY FOR PEOPLE LIVING BELOW THE BAR

TEXT: "Jonathan, Saul's son, had a son who was lame in both feet. He was five years old when the news about Saul and Jonathan came from Jezreel; and his nurse took him up and fled. And it happened, as she made haste to flee, that he fell and became lame. His name was Mephibosheth…"

"Now David said, 'Is there still anyone who is left of the house of Saul, that I may show him kindness for Jonathan's sake?' And there was a servant of the house of Saul whose name was Ziba. So when they had called him to David, the king said to him, 'Are you Ziba?' He said, 'At your service!' Then the king said, 'Is there anyone of the house of Saul, to whom I may show the kindness of God?' And Ziba said to the king, 'There is still as son of Jonathan who is lame in his feet.' So the king said to him, 'Where is he?' And Ziba said to the king, 'Indeed he is in the house of Machir the son of Ammiel, from Lo Debar.' Now when Mephibosheth the son of Jonathan, the son of Saul, had come to David, he fell on his face and prostrated himself. Then David said, 'Mephibosheth?' And he answered, 'Here is your servant!' So David said to him, 'Do not fear, for I will surely show you kindness for Jonathan your father's sake, and will restore to you all the land of Saul your grandfather; and you shall eat bread at my table continually.' Then he bowed himself, and said, 'What is your servant, that you should look upon such a dead dog as I?' And the king called to Ziba, Saul's servant, and said to him, 'I have given to your master's son all that belonged to Saul and to all his house.'" (2Samuel 4:4; 9:1-13, NKJV).

There's a song once lifted by the faithful bards of the past, "Serving the Lord will Pay Off after 'While." I do not know the exact context in which the song was composed or what raw materials of life inspired its writing, but it seems to have been composed in the refinery of difficulty. It seems that someone, while in the midst of great difficulty, had given their all to be faithful to God. Yet they held to the belief of some compensating blessing in the distant horizon. Clearly, the song was composed for a community who shared in the testimony of serving God when they currently had very little to show for it. They were people who were living below the bar of social privileges, people who lacked access to common social benefits.

I do not question the veracity of the song, nor the times in which the song was rendered. I believe that there are persons who have sought to give their all to the Lord and longed for some after-awhile compensation. However, that has not been the case for many of us. Serving the Lord has paid off for many of us! I know that I have been immeasurably blessed in the service of the Lord. Since I began earnestly serving the Lord, I have seen more, gone to more places, met more people, engaged in more exhilarating experiences, and even had a few dollars placed in my care. The inheritance that I will leave my children will be more testimony than treasure, but serving the Lord has paid off.

I remember a conversation between the black students of my graduating class and our senior advisor, Dr. Peter Paris. As we were preparing to exit Vanderbilt University, Dr. Paris informed us, upon receipt of the Master of Divinity Degree, that we would be entering middle class. I thought it strange of him to be speaking of social status, when all I really wanted to do was to give my life in the service of God for my people. In fact, I resented his statement. I knew from where the Lord had brought me, and it was to those living below the bar that I wanted to do ministry. I believe that the blessed of God are called to minister to people who live below the bar. I yet believe that our most impactful ministries are those that touch the lives of people who live below the bar of social privileges, to people who lack access to common social benefits.

Here I am, 25 years later, back in Richmond, still concerned with ministry for people who are living below the bar. I've had the opportunity to serve people with significant wealth and privilege, but my heart remains for the people below the bar. I ran from a so-called bourgeois congregation when a sister on the pulpit committee invited me and my then-wife to visit her to see her Chinese art. I thought, oh how disconnected - an African American woman living in a house filled with Chinese art! There are some who envy my opportunity to serve the Bethlehem Missionary Baptist Church, but I know that my heart beats for doing ministry among those below the bar.

> A point of sensitivity for people in today's church is to know that many of the people who now live below the bar have been crippled because someone dropped them.

Yet, when I read the episode in David's life with Mephibosheth, I am challenged to reassess what it means to minister to people below the bar. The Bible tells us that David's best friend, Jonathan, son of his worst enemy, Saul, had a son named Mephibosheth. Mephibosheth was born into royalty, but when the political and economic tides turned for the worse, he was literally and figuratively dropped from a position of privilege to a life below the bar. The child's world had taken a tragic turn because of the death of Saul and Jonathan. The nurse, a responsible caregiver, picked up baby Mephibosheth, and while running for their lives, she dropped him and he became crippled in both feet.

A point of sensitivity for people in today's church is to know that many of the people who now live below the bar have been crippled because someone dropped them. The swelling numbers of young people filling up juvenile detention centers, mental health institutions, foster care, drug houses, whorehouses, crack corners, and hot prostitution spots are the people who have been dropped. People who were their designated caregivers were running from some family-related disaster, and while carrying the young, dropped them. That poor sister in the South being charged with child abuse because of her son's obesity is like so many poor people who have nothing to give children but fattening food. A lot of children are in the house with their alleged caregivers and being dropped into poor diets; dropped into toxic family systems; dropped into generational poverty; and dropped into the abyss of crippling social challenges.

The caregivers are not evil and probably not bad people. I suspect that many of them mean well, but life has been known to set some people on the run. People have been known to run from fearful circumstances, shame, guilt, abuse, and endless cycles of violence. In their run for their own safety, and the safety of children, children sometimes get dropped and become socially and emotionally crippled. I hold that there are not a lot of downright evil people in the world, but a lot of the people we call 'bad' have been dropped, crippled, and damaged.

I do not know how long it was before David became concerned about his best friend's children; the text doesn't say. However, it was long enough for David to become acclimated to privilege and detached from the people below the bar. I'm bothered by David's query. David asked, "Is there still anyone who is left of the house of Saul, that I may show him kindness for Jonathan's sake?"

Some of you may think it a noble thing for David to want to be kind to his enemy's family. Jesus said, "Bless those who despitefully use you." Yet, when you read the text, David's desire is to be kind for Jonathan's sake. Jonathan was his best friend, his homey, his cut-buddy, his road dog. David bothers me because he should have known where Mephobisheth was, even if he was living below the bar. Two of my dear friends died rather young and left children behind. I know the exact locations of Ralph's and Marvis' children. I know exactly where PJ, Crystal,

> *Have we become so isolated in church that we don't know where the marginalized people are?*

Stacy, Chantel, and Nicholas are. Furthermore, I want to believe that they know that if they need anything, they can call me.

David ought to trouble some of us, because too many of us at BMBC are out of touch with people below the bar. We've become acclimated to the blessings of God in our lives and busy with self-gratifying church work. David troubles me further because he doesn't even know where Lodebar is, or who's keeping Lodebar. He's totally out of touch with marginalized people and the institutional systems that keep them living below the bar.

Have we become so isolated in church that we don't know where the marginalized people are? I suspect that the bullets whizzing through the air in Richmond are gun shots from Lodebar. Lodebar is the place of institutional marginalization, where people are placed within the margins of society. People who are living below the bar are confined to certain areas where the mentality of Lodebar can be developed and maintained. Lodebar is where you end up when dropped by caregivers and assigned by society to live among people who are going nowhere.

And there is always a Machir, a system of oppression that keeps people in Lodebar. Tim Wise in his wonderful book, Between Barak and A Hard Place, argues that just because Obama has been elected president doesn't mean that America has stopped being racist. He pleads to white folks that they not buy into the new racism where blacks, like Obama, are accepted when they are exceptional, educated, and articulated, while the rest remain under suspicion. I pray that Obama knows that a beer in the White House does not take away the sting of being dehumanized, just because you look like someone who lives below the bar.

Machir is not interested in developing jobs, reviving the economy, building affordable housing, providing affordable health care, keeping schools open, and shutting down jails. No! Machir is only interested in keeping people below the bar in Lodebar. And Machir's work is made easy when the people of God have no clue how to minister to people below the bar.

The late Earnest T. Campbell, pastor of Riverside Church, once said, "Before the truth sets us free, it must first make us mad." David's detachment bothers me, but his consequent actions encourage me. Unlike so many of us, David does not stay stuck in the comforts of his privileges. He opens up a window of opportunity to minister to people below the bar.

Again, I have more Bible than I have sermon. Yet, indulge me to lift up a few challenges in this text that make powerful suggestions about how to minister to people below the bar. David's desire to bless someone for Jonathan's sake, who happens to be of the house of Saul, involves the house of Saul. Ziba, a servant of the house of Saul, comes forth and tells David about Mephibosheth, where he is, and who's in charge of his location.

To minister to people below the bar calls for allies. To gain information about the whereabouts of people with whom David was disconnected, he needed an ally. I've been here for three years and I've been noting who joins our church and who sticks around. The people who join and stick around are usually people like us, people living near the bar, or even above the bar. Very few below-the-bar people stick around Bethlehem, and if the truth be told, some of us don't want them to stick around. We want show-off members, folk above the bar.

The people who most need the gospel, who are most receptive to the gospel, and who will benefit the most from the gospel are those below the bar. The ministry of Jesus was meant to include people below the bar: the poor, the brokenhearted, the captives, the blind, the broken, the dropped, and the oppressed. Since we don't seem to have a clue about how to minister to people below the bar, we might need to consider some allies. There are some people in Richmond, in California, in America, who may not operate from the same faith perspective as us, but they know about Lodebar. They know where Mephibosheth, the dropped of life, are located.

They may not have a gospel to preach, a Bible to read, a song to sing, or a church to recommend, but they know the people below the bar. Some of you read my article, Silent Clergy. I suspect the clergy are silent in Richmond because they don't want to be exposed for not knowing about Lodebar. They don't want to be placed in a place of vulnerability where clergy inadequacies will show up.

What the Zibas in life can do is to teach us what we need to know about Lodebar. There are some things we need to learn, some tools we need to be equipped with, in order to effectively minister to people below the bar. I wonder, sometimes, why we think we know everything. We can learn from other people, and they don't need to know the Bible to teach us something.

The second thing that David did was to expose himself to the pain of Mephibosheth. When Mephibosheth came before

David, he fell before David, and cried, "What is your servant, that you should look upon such a dead dog as I?" David wanted to bless the young man with a great blessing, but the young man had been so dehumanized that he was in no shape to receive a blessing. He not only saw himself as a dog, but as a dead dog.

> *Church folk have a hard time being exposed to the pain of broken, damaged, and dehumanized people.*

It's not easy to expose ourselves to the pain of other people, particularly those below the bar. Church folk have a hard time being exposed to the pain of broken, damaged, and dehumanized people. Before people can get out the extent of their pain, we start trying to fix them with some impotent Baptist prescription, which really isn't relevant to where they are, or who they are. Perhaps, we can't take the exposure of other people's pain, because it might expose our inadequacies. Yet, it's in the pain of the broken where ministry comes forth, not from the impotent prescriptions of the whole. The Bible said, "He was wounded for our transgressions, bruised for our iniquity, and the chastisement of our peace was on him."

Jesus exposed Himself to our pain before He was able to heal our pain. He was hurt before He helped. He died, and then was raised. Ministering to people below the bar calls for us to sit with people in the pain of their story.

David bothered me, but he also blessed me by showing me that ministering to those below the bar requires allies, a willingness to be exposed to the pain of others, but also a willingness to give beyond duty and expectation. David blessed Mephibosheth with resources beyond his expectations, but he also invited him to sit at his table for the rest of his life. He gave Mephibosheth adequate resources to live like a king, but he also gave him a place at the table of the King.

> *To minister to those below the bar is to bless people while they are crippled, while they are lame, while they are struggling.*

What blows my mind is not what David did, but when he did it! David didn't wait until Mephibosheth was healed, straightened out, completely recovered, got off probation, got clean. No! He blessed him while he was crippled. The chapter concludes by making note, "So Mephibosheth dwelt in Jerusalem, for he ate continually at the king's table. And he was lame in both his feet."

To minister to those below the bar is to bless people while they are crippled, while they are lame, while they are struggling. If you don't see how to do it in the lives of others, then think of what the Lord did for you. "While we were yet sinners, Christ died for us."

I don't know about you, but the Lord blessed me while I was crippled, while I was below the bar. In fact, I still am not all that I could be, but the Lord keeps blessing me anyhow. The reason I praise God is because I know that my presence at His table was not because I've been so good, did everything right, or that I was able to pick myself up. I've been blessed to be at His table, because God is a good God. I know from where I've come, and I'm glad to be where I am, but it's all because of Him. I should still be in Lodebar, but here I am, praising His name. HALLELUJAH! PRAISE HIS NAME!

REFLECTIONS

1. When looking at your congregation, what issues of class and privilege dominate? Name them.

2. Do you know the places in your community where people have been assigned to living below the bar?

3. What are the current social issues that hinder the above people from having access to normal/standard social benefits?

4. Create a space and place where you and your congregation and/or organization can strategize on how to partner with those within the community who live below the bar.

Chapter 10
PIMPING PAIN: The Irony of Community Compassion
By Reverend Dr. Alvin C. Bernstine

NOTE: The following article was submitted for publication in the local papers in 2010, as a response to the apparent exploitation of the continuing violence in Richmond. It had become near comic as entity after entity positioned for resources to address the violence, when in fact, nothing being suggested had a record of abating urban violence. I could almost hear the "boys" in the hood saying, "That's pimpin' !"

It is with painful irony that I cite some of the current reactions to the violence being perpetuated within the city of Richmond. It seems that many are using the pain of people as opportunities to advance selfish agendas. This would not be so painful if it was limited to the normal suspects, but it has become the exploitative norm for many persons and institutions that should really be "bearing the infirmities of the weak." There is a certain irony in the compassionate expressions of those who are alleging concern. The irony smacks of one of the world's oldest social exploits – pimping.

Pimping represents economic exploitation, under the disguise of having the exploited party's best interest at heart. It is a cruel psychological game where the weakness of one is leveraged for the grandiose enrichment of another. Pimping actually uses the pain of one party to bring economic gain to another. The pimped take all the risks and the pimp gets all the benefits and accompanying glory. The pimped often believe that the pimp has their best interests at heart, even if the outcomes are in extreme contradiction. The pimped are made to believe that there is something compassionate about the arrangements and activities of the pimp.

> *Pimping represents economic exploitation, under the disguise of having the exploited party's best interest at heart.*

This is eerily what I am seeing in Richmond. The political leaders are actually using the senseless violence in Richmond as either campaign rhetoric or opportunities to enrich their coffers and leverage political opportunity. It appears that the pain of the people is being used by some politicians to seek funding for programs that are not working, have never worked and will never work. Millions of dollars are being pumped into Richmond but have no credible impact on the painful plight of the citizenry in the lowlands of Richmond. If one lives in North Richmond, which is a section considered unincorporated, the pain is intensified. This is a cruel act of exploitation, using the pain of oppressed people as the means for advancing political careers, doing it all in the name of alleged compassion.

Another example is the Richmond Police Department. The Richmond Police Department is receiving millions of dollars, and police are working countless hours of overtime, while perpetrators of violence act whenever they want and wherever they want. Police who don't live in the city are running up the clock on the city, while the violence goes unabated within the city. I do not seek to minimize the presence and practice of dedicated police. There are many wonderful police, who put their lives on the line for this city every day . Yet, there are too many police who will be retiring on the violence of Richmond, and when they retire, the violence will continue. This is also a cruel act of exploitation, using the pain of the people as a means of securing economic well-being, while the well-being of the people is negated in the name of "serve and protect."

I've watched in total amazement as leaders of non-profit organizations pimp the pain of the people for funding opportunities for largely impotent organizations. Certainly, there is a need for community-based organizations, but not as mere disguises for personal enrichment. Clearly, the violence in Richmond provides ample opportunities for grand-standing a false concern, while the ultimate goal is to seek funding to finance social pipe-dreams. Nowhere is this more evident than in the so-called African American-led organizations that have to compete among themselves for dwindling financial support. Yet, the funding of an organization should not be the paramount concern when young people's lives are being destroyed. Richmond can be better served when life-saving goals become the aim of funding, and not just the justification of an ill-managed, self-promoting non-profit organization. When the violence in

Richmond is used as fodder for funding, then that is a cruel act of pimping the pain of ill-served people.

The local and national media has pimped the pain of Richmond for ratings, which ultimately stimulates commercial sponsors. When the only news about Richmond seems to be the next senseless act of violence, then the vitality of the city is ignored and the pain of the people is exploited. Richmond is more than violence, rapes, and angry, misguided youths. Richmond represents a wonderful community that has historically been exploited by predators of every stripe. The local and national news does a disservice to Richmond when the only broadcasted news is bad news. I believe a journalistic exposé of Richmond would reveal a pattern of exploitation, not uncommon in urban America, where the pain of a particular community is maintained to sustain the greedy exploits of another community. The media has a responsibility to report the whole story, and not just the parts that feed a frenzy of fear and community terror. When media focuses exclusively upon a people's pain, the result is a cruel example of pimping the pain of people for that which does not help the people.

> *Richmond represents a wonderful community that has historically been exploited by predators of every stripe.*

Another more painful exploitation of the violence in Richmond is in the ministry. Although the ministers of the city have responded in admirable numbers, their responses are tainted by strong efforts to impose individual and personal agendas, as well as untimely and misguided efforts to proselytize. Some of this may result from a lack of clarity on the nature of this violence, but too much comes out that speaks of a desire to be seen, recognized, validated, and promoted. No church, pastor, minister or ministry should be using the pain of our moments to advance a selfish agenda. To do so is a cruel and insensitive effort to pimp the pain of our people, and to shamelessly do it in the name of God.

What Richmond needs is a movement of compassion that will respond to the pain of our people. We need people guided by compassion with a view toward alleviating the pain, not sustaining the pain. The only thing that can transform the vicious cycle of senseless violence that is being afflicted upon this city is for all of us to locate compassion within, and to exercise this compassion in ways that will significantly change the conditions that are giving rise to the violence.

We can pimp this moment as a kind of miniature Katrina-response, where billions of unaccounted-for dollars were sent into New Orleans to help people. Yet, even as I write this, the areas that were most painfully devastated by Katrina have not been rebuilt and the people who were most pained by the experience are still displaced. Richmond cannot represent some civic whore where predators are enriched by her inability to adequately address her pain. We have a responsibility to redeem our people, not pimp our people.

REFLECTIONS

1. What are your feelings and understandings about the practice of pimping?

2. Do you see ways in which the practice of pimping can be duplicated in other social arenas and by so-called law-abiding citizenry?

3. Who are the major players against violence in your community?

4. Create a space and place where your congregation and/or organization can discuss evidence-based programs that address urban violence.

Chapter 11
"A BROTHER ON THE WAY"

TEXT: "Now they came to Jericho. As He went out of Jericho with His disciples and a great multitude, blind Bartimaeus, the son of Timaeus, sat by the road begging. And when he heard that it was Jesus of Nazareth, he began to cry out and say, 'Jesus, Son of David, have mercy on me!' Then many warned him to be quiet; but he cried out all the more, 'Son of David, have mercy on me!' So Jesus stood still and commanded him to be called. Then they called the blind man, saying to him, 'Be of good cheer. Rise, He is calling for you.' And throwing aside his garment, he arose and came to Jesus. So Jesus answered and said to him, 'What do you want me to do for you?' The blind man said to him, 'Rabonni, that I may receive my sight.' Then Jesus said to him, 'Go your way; your faith has made you well.' And immediately he received his sight and followed Jesus on the road" (Mark 10:46-52, NKJV).

Of the many truths that God has shown me, none has been as prominent as the healing of our people through the healing of men. Of all the people who will impact the healing of our people, the health of men looms large. A healthy man can bring health to a bent or broken woman. A healthy man will know how to get healing for children who are filled with hell. A healthy man will bring a sense of order and health to our communities. A healthy man will do healthy things to bring healing to our nation. Men of health are eager to serve the Lord and will bring ceaseless praise to God, because a healthy man knows that his health and help comes from the Lord. The challenge of today's message is for us to do all we can to get the brothers on the way toward living life in ways that are healthy.

In my travels around the globe, the memories that are seared in my head and heart are not the great monuments, castles, or cathedrals. What is seared in my head and heart are images of poor children rushing to me with outstretched hands, seeking a response from the destitution that is so much a part of their lives. In most cases, the children who represented the destitute masses were children of color.

As I prayerfully mused and struggled over what God wanted in today's message, I had an unusual experience. After nearly thirty years of trying to preach, for the first time, I had a whole lot of once-broken brothers within the Bible rushing forth like those children, with outstretched hands wanting to help me preach to the brothers. Each brother had been made well from a condition that finds expression in men today.

The Bible is filled with men whose lives were inhibited by social, systemic,

> *The Bible is filled with men whose lives were inhibited by social, systemic, and internalized disease, before God showed up and helped the brother get on the way.*

and internalized disease, before God showed up and helped the brother get on the way. Naaman, a man of status and acclaim, was a leper. He held up his hand and sought to help me preach to brothers about facing the weaknesses that overshadow our strengths. Mephibosheth, the club-footed brother, held up his hand. He wanted to testify about how God can pick you up when society has let you down. The Gaderene grave dweller, who had severe control issues, wanted to help me preach to brothers about being delivered from multiple evil spirits. The man by the pool for thirty-eight years, with his bed still in his hand, wanted to speak about the futility of living life in the bed. The man whose hand was withered held up his once-withered hand and said, "I can give a powerful testimony about living with no sense of power." Zachariah spoke from a tree about what God can do with a man with small-man complex. Lazarus made a compelling plea to testify to us about dead men walking. However, Bartimaeus won out. The Lord said to let Bartimaeus speak, because his condition is quite common among men in the church. Bartimaeus can help us get brothers on the way.

As Jesus made His way to Jerusalem, they went through Jericho. On His way out of Jericho, a multitude of people followed, but a man on the side of the road stood out. The text says, "Blind Bartimaeus, the son of Timaeus, sat by the road begging." Here was a man who was identified by two things that caused him to do one thing. He was noted as being blind. He could not see. He was also noted as being the son of Timaeus. In fact, his name Bartimaeus means, "Son of Timaeus." Yet, Timaeus was not someone with whom anyone wanted to be identified. Timaeus literally means, "unclean" or "stinking".

Bartimaeus means "Son of the stinking man."

Bartimaeus had a noted physical disability, compounded with a negative social stigma, which pushed him to the roadsides of life where he begged. I cannot help but see a condition that characterizes so many brothers in America. In America, many brothers have internalized the lie that something must be physically wrong with being black, and this lie is compounded with a negative social stigma that causes us to hate our ancestors; as a result, we live our lives begging. Like blindness, being black in America cannot be hidden, nor can we escape the negative stigma placed upon those who birthed us.

> *This society has diseased us with a hatred of black fatherhood.*

We don't announce it, but the way that we always live on the sidelines highly suggests that we believe something is wrong with us and that something was wrong with our fathers. This society has diseased us with a hatred of black fatherhood. We see it all the time! Let a professional athlete do well and get a microphone in his mouth. The first thing he will express is love for his mother, and he'll identify his father as having nothing to do with his life. How does he think he got here? Black folk don't have test tube babies. The killings in our communities are by boys who believe that something is wrong with them, compounded by the hatred for patriarchal ancestry. A defining sociological characteristic of at-risk youth is the absence of a father, no patriarchal influence.

Some of you are probably asking what that has to do with you. I used the essence of Bartimaeus' plight to set us up for the real issue in the text. Skip with me to verse 51. Jesus asked Bartimaeus, "What do you want Me to do for you?" The blind man said to Him, "Rabboni, that I may receive my sight."

The last time Jesus asked that question was in verse 36, when James and John ambushed him with special requests. The story of Bartimaeus comes at the conclusion of a chapter where Jesus struggled with the blindness of His disciples. The disciples could not see where children fit into the program of the kingdom. Jesus said, "I say to you whoever does not receive the kingdom of God as a little child will by no means enter it." The disciples could not see the true cost of following Jesus. Jesus said, "Assuredly, I say to you, there is no one who has left house or brothers or sisters or father or mother or children or lands, for my sake and gospel's who shall not receive a hundredfold now in this time – and in the age to come." The disciples could not see having access to the kingdom without having special seats and privileges. Jesus said, "And whoever of you desires to be first shall be slave of all. For even the Son of Man did not come to be served, but to serve, and to give His life a ransom for many."

The real state of blindness is in those who claim to be close to Jesus. The brothers who claim to know Him lack clarity, and for that, they are not on the way. They are in the way. Whenever Christian men lack vision and compassion for children, and are more into silver and gold, big seats, and special privileges, they are not on the way, but are in the

> *The brothers who claim to know Him lack clarity, and for that, they are not on the way. They are in the way.*

way. If such disease or blindness exists in church brothers, imagine the intensity of blindness among men outside the church.

However, Bartimaeus helps us to see how to get brothers on the way. When Jesus asked Bartimaeus what He could do for him, Bartimaeus knew exactly what he wanted. He answered, "Rabboni, that I may receive my sight." One of the things that Bartimaeus helps us understand is that in order for Jesus to something for us, He must first do something with us. Yet, what Jesus must do with us depends upon clarity from us.

> *One of the things that Bartimaeus helps us understand is that in order for Jesus to do something for us, He must first do something with us.*

Bartimaeus knew exactly what he needed done to him. He does not point to anything external to himself. He does not tell Jesus to fix the world, the community, the schools, other people, or the church. He said, "That I might receive my sight."

Brothers, we are truly blind when we don't know what Jesus can do for us. The one authentic reason why many of us are here is because we know that we need Jesus to do something for us. All of us have some unique issue that we need to be honest about. We cannot get on the way unless we first address what it is about us that keeps getting in our way. If it's in our way, then it's in the way of our children. If it's in our way, then it's in the way of our relationships with women. If it's in our way, then it's in the way of our Christian witness. If it's in our way, then it's in the way of our worship. We can't serve or worship

God if we are not being real about what's in our way.

How do we get to Bartimaeus' clarity? The first thing that leaps from the text is that Bartimaeus does not allow the things that are wrong with him to disable the things that were right with him. He was blind. He had a bad name. Yet, he could still talk. When he heard that it was Jesus of Nazareth, he began to cry out and say, "Jesus, Son of David, have mercy on me!"

He had heard about Jesus, and when Jesus came close, he used what he had to get Jesus' attention. I just believe that we can get more brothers on the way if more of us would quit focusing on what's wrong with us, and use what is right with us. The one thing we can do is make some noise! All the noise we make at a ballgame when someone hits a homerun, scores a bucket, or makes a touchdown. We, brothers, ought to be ashamed to be so quiet when the Lord is near. We ought to make some noise! Get the Lord's attention, and ask the Lord to have mercy on us!

The second thing he does is persist when the crowed resisted. The Bible says, "Then many warned him to be quiet; but he cried out all the more, Son of David, have mercy on me!" The crowd sought to resist him, to restrain him, to quiet him down. Instead of resigning to the wishes of the crowd, Bartimaeus persisted in seeking the mercy of Christ.

What keeps so many brothers from getting on the way is that we let people get in our way. We give up on dreams by resigning to crowd pressure. We miss our moment by allowing people to limit us. We miss out on what God wants to do for us, by allowing the crowd to quiet us. I have often said that most of the brothers who are being hindered by drugs, jail, and other destructive behavior would be hugely blessed just by changing crowds.

Some of us need to get real, today, and decide that we are ready to live above the crowd. Some brother needs to get real, and decide to go where the crowd won't go and don't want me or you to go. For men to get on the way, we have to persist when the crowd resists. We have to believe that our blessing is not in the crowd, but in Christ.

The Bible says, "So Jesus stood still and commanded him to be called. Then they called the blind man, saying to him, ' Be of good cheer. Rise, He is calling you.'" Notice, if you will, that when the man came to Jesus and was asked what Jesus could do for him, He answered. Jesus never touched the man. He never told the brother to go wash in a pool. Jesus didn't make eye salve from mud, and place it on the brother's eyes. In fact, all Jesus said, "'Go your way; your faith has made you well.' And immediately he received his sight and followed Jesus on the way."

Jesus told the brother, "Go your way, your faith has made you well." Yet, the only way Bartimaeus could go was the Jesus way. He immediately followed Jesus on the way. He didn't go back to the roadside. He didn't go back to begging. He didn't go back to his old lifestyle . He decided to go the Jesus way.

Someone needs to hear me this morning, because the Lord doesn't heal you to go your own way. When the Lord brings healing to you, the only way to go is the Jesus way. The Lord doesn't bless you to go your way. When the Lord blesses you, the only way to go is the Jesus way. For if the Lord is merciful enough to open your eyes, good sense ought to tell you that you haven't seen anything yet.

If you go the Jesus way, then the Lord will show out along the way. Go the Jesus way, and you may go by the Cross, see Him nailed, crucified, buried, and placed in a tomb. Go the Jesus way, and on the other side of the tomb, you'll see a resurrection morning. Go the Jesus way, and He will show you that He has all the power of heaven and earth in His hand.

I don't know about you, but I have decided to follow Jesus - no turning back, no turning back. HALLELUJAH! PRAISE HIS NAME!

REFLECTION

1. What are your thoughts on the challenges of living in America with a physical disability compounded with a social stigma?

2. Can you list some ways in which fatherhood has been demonized in the African American community?

3. Identify some serious areas of ministry blindness in your current congregation.

4. Create a context where your congregation and/or organization can explore ways in which to empower African American men to use the power(s) that is available to them.

Chapter 12
THE GOSPEL FOR THE GHETTO

TEXT: "So the child grew and was weaned. And Abraham made a great feast on the same day Isaac was weaned. And Sarah saw the son of Hagar the Egyptian, whom she had borned to Abraham, scoffing. Therefore she said to Abraham, 'Cast out this bondwoman and her son; for the son of this bondwoman shall not be heir with my son, namely with Isaac.' And the matter was very displeasing in Abraham's sight because of his son. But God said to Abraham, 'Do not let it be displeasing in your sight because of the lad or because of the bondwoman. Whatever Sarah has said to you, listen to her voice; for in Isaac your see shall be called. Yet I will also make a nation of the son of the bondwoman, because he is your seed.' So Abraham rose early in the morning, and took bread and a skin of water; and putting it on her shoulder, he gave it and the boy to Hagar, and sent her away. Then she departed and wandered in the Wilderness of Beersheba. And the water in the skin was used up, and she placed the boy under one of the shrubs. Then she went and sat down across from him at a distance of about a bowshot; for she said to herself, 'Let me not see the death of the boy.' So sat opposite him, and lifted her voice and wept. And God heard the voice of the lad. Then the angel of God called to Hagar out of heaven and said to her, 'What ails you, Hagar? Fear not, for God has heard the voice of the lad where he is. Arise, lift up the lad and hold him with your hand, for I will make him a great nation.' Then God opened her eyes, and she saw a well of water. And she went and filled the skin with water, and gave the lad a drink. So God was with the lad; and he grew and dwelt in the wilderness, and became an archer. He dwelt in the Wilderness of Paran; and his mother took a wife for him from Egypt" (Genesis 21:8-21, NKJV).

The primary goal in all that the church does is to set forth good news. In fact, we are under the obligation to be bearers of good news. Our gatherings on Sunday and all we do during the week are to be an expression of good news. The good news responsibility of the church may be expressed in many ways, but critical to our good news burden is to be faithful to the Bible. Unless we change into some Post-Modern cult, the Bible represents the primary source from which we present the good news of Jesus Christ to the world.

However, as I continue to expose myself to the truths of the Bible, the Bible has exposed some unsettling truths to me. One of the latest exposures of biblical truth is that the Bible often contains good news from the context of a bad-news world. It's a strange mixture of God's grace being revealed within the space of our disgrace.

A case in point is the story of our text. The story of our text is surrounded by good news which is set within the context of a world of bad news. The good news of the text is the birth of Isaac. The good news of the text is God using people beyond the boundaries of human capacity. The good news of the text is God's promises overriding human expectation. The good news of the text is that God brings new life in death-like situations. The good news of the text is a future in the face of human failure. The good news of the text is that "with God all things are possible." However, the bad news of the text is the use of privilege and power to exile a woman and child from the vicinity of blessings. God's grace exposes the atrocities within the space of human disgrace.

> *God is so awesome that He offers good news to people who are forced to live in a bad-news world, even the world of the ghetto.*

Sarah, who laughed at the opening of the chapter, used her privilege and power to ban Hagar and Ishmael from having access to resources. The bad news was that she did not want Ishmael in the vicinity of the blessings of Isaac. The bad news is how people who are blessed can sometimes be so small, and will use the privileges of their blessings to deprive powerless people. The news gets worse, because the text also suggests that God somehow sanctions the exile of Hagar and Ishmael. (I know a lot of brothers who, like Abraham, think that what their wives say must be the voice of God.) However, the good news is that God knows about people who have been assigned to places of scarce resources. God is so awesome that He offers good news to people who are forced to live in a bad-news world, even the world of the ghetto.

The healing that is needed for our people must also be from negative social constructs. The bad news of our world is that there exist social constructs that empower some people to assign other people to live away from wealth and privileges. Just as in the Bible, there are negative realities that allow some people to adversely affect the lives of other people. Wherever people's lives are disrupted and forced to live with meager resources, a ghetto is created.

Historically, the ghetto did not begin with black people. Historically, the ghetto began with the European persecution of the Jews. Ghettos were created when Jews were forced to live in certain areas and made to live off meager resources. Placing the Jews within despicable living conditions substantiated the hatred of the Jews by forcing them to live in inhumane conditions. Black people originally used the term "ghetto" to show parallels between our living conditions and the persecuted Jews. It was a sociological term used during the civil rights struggle by the proponents of black power. However, as most things black, we romanticized the word and it became an accepted stigma for where and how black people live. We embraced and internalized that which characterized our own oppression.

The ghetto has become the norm for where African Americans live. It describes a place of social deprivation where certain people are made to live off meager resources. In reality, it becomes a place where people are set up to die. Basic sociology teaches that where you live determines how you will die and what you will die from.

Hagar and Ishmael were banished from the vicinity of blessings, and were given bread and a skin of water. She was sent away with just meager resources and she wandered in the

Wilderness of Beersheba. The bread ran out and the water dried up. She set the boy under a shrub, and she distanced herself from him. She said, "'Let me not see the death of the boy.' So she sat opposite him, and lifted her voice and wept."

> *We are healed from within and not from without.*

As sympathetic as I am toward Hagar, she challenges us. She challenges us to look at the ghettozation of black America. She challenges us to see that our healing comes not from where we are, but who we are. If we see where we are as a place of death, then we see ourselves as people who are dying. Let me put it another way: although we live in the ghetto, we can't let the ghetto live in us. We are healed from within and not from without.

What has happened to many of our people is that we can be out of the ghetto, but yet live the ghetto as a person. We have internalized a ghetto perspective on life, and we do what the young people call going "ghetto." When the ghetto lives in you, you believe that the best stuff is always somewhere else. When the ghetto lives in you, then the best privileges, the best opportunities, the best future, the best way of living are always somewhere other than where you are. Hagar went ghetto and believed that the best opportunity, the best privileges, the best future, and the best way of life were in the camp among people who would kick her out.

I believe that we need healing from being ghetto fabulous, but people need serious healing when they believe that they have made it, they have arrived, when they are closer to people who will kick them out. Something is wrong with people who will commute a hundred miles a day to live among people who would kick them out. Aunt Hagar's children need healing because we are worse than ghetto fabulous - we are ghetto-rageous.

> *I'm moved by the suggestion of this text, because maybe our healing will not come from crying mothers but from praying children.*

Yet the good news of the ghetto is that while God hears crying, He listens to prayers. Hagar was sitting down crying, despairing, and waiting for death. Ishmael was praying. The Bible does not tell us what he prayed, or even how he prayed. The Bible simply tells us, "God has heard the voice of the lad where he is." Here is the silence of the biblical text. It doesn't speak of the human reality, only the divine response. While Hagar was crying in the ghetto, Ishmael was praying from the ghetto, and the good news is that God heard him right where he was.

Some of you need to hear this word, because your healing depends on you shifting from crying, complaining, and despairing in the ghetto to lifting up prayer from the ghetto. It might be the place where we are desolate and despairing, but never let the desolation and despair take root in our spirits. It might be a place where we are deprived, but scarceness of resources never limits God.

I'm moved by the suggestion of this text, because maybe our healing will not come from crying mothers but from praying children. If some of our children will put down the guns, quit the cussing and dissing, and start praying, then we'll quit waiting on death and start looking for new life. The lad's praying moved God, and in the process got Hagar moving. God said, "Arise, lift up the lad and hold him with your hand for I will make him a great nation."

> When we start acting differently, God will show us something different.

A prayer movement in young people could erase some of this distance between parents and children. This is no time for our children to be in one place and parents in another place. Even if your situation is like Hagar's, a single parent, you need to be within lifting range of your children. They may look big, act grown, fast, and mannish, but they need adults to lift them up and hold them in their hands. Much of this bizarre behavior can be healed if some adults would get close enough to care, close enough to touch, and care enough to lift.

When she lifted up Ishmael, the Bible says, "Then God opened her eyes, and she saw a well of water." When she lifted, God opened. When she acted, God revealed. God did not make new water. There was no stream that miraculously appeared. The water was there all the time. Her move to do something different gave God an opportunity to show her something different.

While she was down in despair, she couldn't see. While she was waiting on death, she could not see the waters of life. When she moved to give life, God showed her new life. God showed her that there is water in the ghetto.

I need someone to hear me on this today. You need to

hear the gospel in the ghetto that tells us that there is life in the ghetto. When we start acting differently, God will show us something different. Our healing depends upon taking responsibility of where we are, so that God can bless us right where we are. We don't have to leave Richmond; God can bless us in Richmond. We don't have to move out of our communities; God can bless us in our community.

"And she went and filled the skin with water, and gave the lad a drink." The Bible says, "So God was with the lad; and he grew and dwelt in the wilderness, and became an archer." Right there in the ghetto, the lad grew and became somebody. He became an archer, someone who hit what he aimed at.

Ain't that good news? God heard the lad where he was, and spoke to the parent where she was. The lad grew where he was. He hit whatever he aimed at. I don't know about you, but I see some healing in this text. I hear some good news for Bethlehem in a bad-news world like Richmond. I hear a word of hope that our children can grow up in Richmond, and hit whatever they aim for.

The reason that God has us here is to lift up some young people and give them something to aim for. In a city where people are waiting to die, the ministry of BMBC is to lift up some young people and give them something to aim for. So my prayer is, "Lord, open our eyes so that we can see water in Richmond." We are here to announce good news for the ghetto.

> "For there is a fountain, filled with blood;
> drawn from Emmanuel's veins.
> Sinners plunge beneath the flood,
> Lose all their guilty stains."

REFLECTION

1. What are your thoughts on the grace of God being expressed within the spaces and places of human disgrace?

2. Can you identify some of the negative social constructs within your community? How are they upheld?

3. In what ways do internalized oppression affect the outlook of people within your community?

4. Create a space and place where your congregation and/or organization can discuss the powerful collaboration between praying youth and the adults who lift them.

Chapter 13
"OVERCOMING VICTIMIZATION:
It Took All That!"

TEXT: **"Joseph called the name of the firstborn Manasseh: 'For God has made me forget all my toil and all my father's house.' And the name of the second he called Ephraim: 'For God has caused me to be fruitful in the land of my affliction'" (Genesis 41:51-52, NKJV).**

My doctoral mentor and preaching guru, the late Dr. Samuel Dewitt Proctor, once noted that there are basically two kinds of people in the world: "those who do and those who are done unto." I don't know if I fully understood what he meant, but I still find it an intriguing observation. I find it intriguing because, as I see it, the world celebrates those who do, and sympathizes with those who are done unto. The world cheers for those who do, and gives charity to those who are done unto. The world seeks to emulate those who do, and avoids those who are done unto. The world builds soaring and stately memorials for those who do, but sets up victim funds for those who are done unto. The world works to remember those who do, but can easily forget those who are done unto.

As I listened to a recent reading of my autobiography, it occurred to me that all of what was being said about me was what I had done, and nothing about what had been

> *The Bible story would lack integrity if all it had were nice stories about the great things people did, and none of the horror and gore about the people who were done unto.*

done unto me, or what I had done unto others. Something triggered inside of me that reminded me that my life story is not just about what I have done, but it is also about what has been done unto me, inclusive of what I have done unto others. For me to be who I am, it didn't just include the good things that I did, but it also included the evil that was done unto me. It took all of that! The betrayals, the disappointments, failures, and misfortunes, all are a part of the package known as Alvin C. Bernstine. My unrest continued because the Bible story informs us that our salvation and healing involves remembering not just what we have done, but also remembering what has been done unto us. It took all of that!

Think with me, my brothers and sisters! The Bible story would lack integrity if all it had were nice stories about the great things people did, and none of the horror and gore about the people who were done unto. What would the story of Cain and Abel be like if Abel had not been done unto? What would the drama of Abraham be like, if Hagar and Ishmael were not done unto? What would the story of Esau and Jacob be like, if Esau had not been done unto? What would the Exodus story be like if the children of Israel had not cried to God because they were done unto? What would the crossing of the river Jordan be like, if there were no stones to remind succeeding generations that they had been done unto? What kind of story of David would we have if it didn't include Beersheba and poor Uriah being done unto? What would the stories of Daniel, Shedrach, Mischach, and Abnedgo be like if there were no incidents of them being done unto? What would the Psaltry be like, if there were no songs of people being done unto? How impoverished the Christian journey would be if there were no songs that sang to the memories of being done unto? Such songs as: "You prepare a table before me in the presence of mine enemies"; "Fret not because of evil doers, nor be envious of the workers of iniquity"; "Deliver me, O Lord, from the hands of evildoers"; "I will lift my eyes to the hills, from whence comes my help, my help comes from the Lord."

Lastly, but not least, what kind of Christian testimony would we have if our Lord and Savior had not been done unto? How would Jesus come off with no Judas, no forsaking disciples, no cruel soldiers, no spineless Pilate, and no rugged cross? There is a sense in which we are called to give redemptive relevance to our stories, even those episodes in our lives when we were done unto, because it took all of that. In fact, the point of today's message is that our healing from negative influences calls us to redemptively remember our experiences of when we were done unto. Our complete healing will come when we begin the work of remembering the wrongs that were done unto us in the right way. Our testimony gains the power it needs when it includes our victimization, because it took all of that to make us who we are and it prepares us for the work that God is now calling for us to do.

The story of our text lifts before us a challenging and critical component of being wholly healed, fully saved, and being fully empowered to be an instrument of redemption. It is an incident in the story of a person, who had risen to a place of great importance and acclaim. Joseph had arrived to the position of being second in command of the wealth and resources of Egypt. His life was enviable. His stature admired, and his influence unquestioned. The brother had arrived. Joseph, for all intents and purposes, had become one of those who do, but his ascent to fortune and fame came at the high cost of being done unto.

Although a favorite of his father, Joseph suffered mental, emotional, and finally physical abuse at the hands of his brothers, which was indirectly caused by his father. His brothers could not accept Joseph, because his dreaming made them uncomfortable. He suffered domestic violence because of the collective issues of those in his household. He was further abused by society, which allowed some people to be exploited for the profit of others. His abuse continued when a woman in power, Potiphar's wife, lied on him because he chose not to satisfy her wandering lusts. As a result, he was cast into the most abusive institution known to men: prison, where he was further victimized, exploited, and isolated. Like Joseph's experience, prison violates the most sacred space of men by intensifying the horror of being done unto. The autobiography of Joseph was

> *The painful truth of life is that, for most, victimization is homegrown.*

not just what he did, but it included the horror and gore of being done unto. It took all of that to get Joseph to the place where he could help you and me to start remembering the wrong that has been done unto us in the right way. We need this witness because we are inclined to remember things the wrong way, or to remember things in ways that continue to hurt us and hurt other people.

I don't know about you, but I don't want to miss my blessing by denying and distorting my story. All of us have episodes in our lives where we have been victimized, done unto. For some of us, it began in the home, where like Esther Philips sang, "Home is where the hatred is, and it might be better if I never went back again." The painful truth of life is that, for most, victimization is homegrown. Home has been the place where many first realized that the world can be an unfriendly place, filled with experiences of painful exploitation, maddening manipulation, poisonous perversions, brutal betrayals, scary isolation, and inherent suffering. All of us are who we are because of what has been done unto us. It took all of that!

As a people, we are who we are because of a legacy of victimization. Even when we don't want to remember the slavery experience, the legacy of slavery keeps showing up. The brutal fact of chattel slavery, Jim Crow, and persistent racial injustices assaults and affects the collective psyche of African American people. I viewed the body of the 18-year-old boy lying shrouded in the streets of North Richmond, and listened to people declare no knowledge of what had happened or why it happened. The silence of the witnesses allowed the legacy of slavery to emerge, where the value of black life is not worth anyone knowing about. As I watched beautiful teenage girls strutting the sidewalks in front of an Oakland church, the legacy of slavery emerged where black womanhood is valued only when her body is a tool for the oppressor's pleasure. In this instance, the oppressor is not a white man, but a sick brother wearing sneakers who is "chili" pimping a sister from a cell phone.

> *We have the uncanny capacity of distorting what happened to us in ways that deform us.*

Allow me the freedom of touching upon a sacred secret of the religious: the story of church life has not been all glory without the gory. For instance, last week, the Catholic Church paid over $600 million to victims of clergy abuse. The black church has its own stories of victimization that need to be told, even BMBC. Some of my most painful experiences have been church experiences, where people of faith became pawns of evil. Yet, if I claim any relationship to the Christian witness, I have to confess that it took all of that to make me who I am and empower me to do what I do.

Some of you may be asking: what has that got to do with me? It may not have anything to do with you, but if you are like me, then you know that stuff done unto us affects us and powerfully influences us. We all remember stuff wrong. We have the uncanny capacity of distorting what happened to us in ways that deform us. There is undeniable proof that the

> *Memories are healed when bad experiences are submerged into the awesome plans of God.*

way we interpret our pain determines our gain, and how we read the stuff that hurt us will shape what's left of us. Some of the most beautiful people in the world are people who experienced being done unto, but remembered it in the right way. Likewise, some of the most miserable and cruelest people in the world are people who were done unto and remembered it wrongly. We need to know that God uses the horror and the gory to shape our story, and the only reason we got good news is because we know about the bad news.

At the height of success, newly married, and handling his business, Joseph reveals to us how he overcame victimization. The Bible says, "And to Joseph were born two sons before the years of famine came, whom Asenath, the daughter of Pot-Pherah priest of On, bore to him. Joseph called the name of the firstborn Manasseh: 'For God has made me forget all of my toil and all my father's house.'"

By naming his son Manasseh, Joseph teaches us that by healing our memories, we open up the possibilities of our future. Memories are healed when bad experiences are submerged into the awesome plans of God. In the Bible, the firstborn son was symbolic of a prosperous future for the family. Sons symbolized a future, and the names given to sons symbolized the quality of the future. Joseph saw, in his firstborn son, the kind of future that God wanted him to have, in spite of all that he had been through. God healed the wounds of Joseph's past and set him up for a wonderful future.

Please be clear that when Joseph declared that God made him forget, it does not mean that the injuries inflicted upon him were erased from his memories. He was not forgetting his toils, or the experiences of his father's house, but he was interpreting them in a way that did not hinder him. Joseph seems to have come to the place where he knew that all he had gone through was in the plan of God. He reshaped the narrative of a painful past into a story of a prosperous future.

Admittedly, I am bothered by Joseph's claim because I am not comfortable with a God who has plans for my suffering. I am not always with this God who allows me to be victimized just to work out His plan. It seems to me that God could do just as well without people suffering, being exploited, oppressed, abused, isolated, and manipulated. Yet, when we look closer at Joseph's story, we see that Joseph's rise to success was not about him, but it was about being used as an instrument to save many people.

God knows that the only way to get selfish people like you and me to feel the pain and suffering of other people is for us to know what pain, suffering, exploitation, oppression, and isolation feels like. A lot of what we go through may hurt us personally, but in God's plan, it's not about us; it's about what God wants to work through us. If the truth is told, some of us who once cried over certain situations are now shouting because we now see that God knew what He was doing. The job you cried over losing, you are now glad that you got out of there. That relationship you once cried over, you are now thanking God for delivering you. That person you once prayed to get away from, you're thanking God for keeping you and allowing you

> God allows blessings to flow through the channels of our difficulties.

to witness a glorious change. That door that was closed in your face allowed you to get to a better place.

Just as it was for Joseph, so it's true for you and me, "What was meant for evil, God meant for good." Therefore, for our memories to be healed, let's not hold grudges, be resentful, negative, vengeful, vindictive, and hateful, but let's use all that we've been through as runways to a powerful and prosperous future. Looking at the evil of our past in ways that are redemptive gives us the testimony that "all things work together for the good of those who love the Lord and are the called according to His purpose."

When we get to the next verse, we see the further healing of Joseph from negative memories. The Bible says, "And the name of the second he called Ephraim: 'For God has caused me to be fruitful in the land of my affliction.'" Joseph helps us to be healed from negative memories by focusing on the blessings from the painful lessons. God used the horror and gore of suffering and abuse to give Joseph a story of being fruitful in the place of his affliction. God used the pain to set me up for my gain.

God not only keeps us during the experiences of victimization, but God blesses us in the very places of victimization. Right there in the places of our greatest pain come our greatest gain. God allows blessings to flow through the channels of our difficulties. Manasseh-like forgetfulness frees us for Ephraim-like blessedness. We can't get to Ephraim-like experiences until we experience Manasseh. We have to know that in spite of all we may have gone through, God kept us in order to bless us.

Yes, I've been through hell, but my future is named Manasseh because God has kept me. I've suffered in my life, but my suffering is not going to keep me from my blessing, because my future is named Manasseh – God has kept me. Life has not always seemed fair, but that's all right; my future is still named Manasseh because God has kept me. I've been through some things, but God has kept me. I've been up and I've been down, right and wrong, but it took all of that to get me to Ephraim, my blessing. But I can't get to my blessing, until I'm sure that I have a future that has been healed from negative memories. I need to claim a future that has been shaped by a Manasseh experience, a healing from negative memories, to get to my Ephraim possibilities. Even now, I need a Manasseh blessing because I don't want anything to keep me from getting to my Ephraim blessing, the blessing in the here-and-now. In fact, let me join with the songwriter:

> I thank God for the mountains,
> Thank God for the valleys,
> I thank Him for the storms
> He's brought me through;
> For if I never had a problem
> I would not know that God could solve them;
> I would not know what trusting God could do.

Yes! "Through it all! Through it all!" It took all of that! HALLELUJAH! PRAISE HIS NAME!

REFLECTION:
1. Give an accurate description of your life based upon what you have done and what has been done unto you.

2. How has the story of your community been remembered?

3. Who does your church attract: doers or those who are done unto?

4. Create a space and place where your congregation and/or organization can discuss the challenges of victimization.

Chapter 14
SILENT CLERGY

NOTE: The following editorial opinion was published in the local papers of the Bay Area in 2009. As stated, it was a response to the pain of sitting in meetings where community issues were being discussed, and listening to the query, "Where are the preachers?" At the time of this writing, the city of Richmond was sinking into the abyss of social pathology. Everything that could go wrong was going wrong, and the systems in place were ill-equipped to make any radical difference. I wrote this editorial with the hope of invigorating the Richmond clergy to come forth en masse and provide a prophetic voice. As of this publication, the call has gone forth largely unanswered.

Years ago, as a graduate student of Vanderbilt Divinity School, I read an intriguing book by James Smart, The Silence of the Bible in the Church. Smart's contention was that the Bible was not the primary voice shaping the life of the church. The church had strangely heeded other voices - such as the voices of its history, culture, and tradition - to give shape to its life and ministry.

Although Smart's position may yet hold serious sway in today's church, the concern of this writing is the strange, almost eerie silence of the clergy in responding to the mounting crises within our communities. As a pastor of nearly 25 years, a minister for 32 years, I am deeply concerned about the glaring absence of responsible clergy during one of the most challenging times within the life of our city, state, country, and world.

Since returning to the Bay Area three years ago, I have heard the constant query of concerned community leadership, asking, "Where is the clergy?" I have had to humbly sit through meeting after meeting, and listen to concerned citizens and leaders anguish over the question, "Where are the preachers?" They were not asking about where our church was, or where any preacher was. They were anguishing over the strange absence and silence of the African American preacher, a once constant voice and presence in the struggle for justice, equality, and liberation for African American people. "Where are the preachers?"

As the flatlands of Richmond sink into a cesspool of violence, crime, and economic despair, the leadership of the clergy is noticeably absent and their voices are appallingly silent. As the communities where our people live, work, and worship have come under the dark siege of senseless violence, rising foreclosures, and neighborhood blight, the clergy voice seems to have been isolated to the sanctuary. Oh yes, we show up in our churches and perform our priestly and pastoral duties, but when the community is being viciously mugged with persistent black-on-black crime, where are the clergy? We seemingly have no capacity for what Dr. J. Alfred Smith, Sr. calls "the ministry of the Jericho road." We are content with "having" church without really "being" the church.

> *Where are the preachers when strategies are needed to redeem our community from the clutches of growing despair?*

Certainly, there is the "chosen" one or two, who seem to have a knack for camera shots and news sound-bites, but the clergy who hold responsibility for the masses of the people are neither heard from nor seen. We may even have "moments" of reactionary assembly, where we march or convene in protest or support, but a consistent presence of prophetic leadership is eerily lacking. Unfortunately, some of us have been seduced by the adoring masses on Sunday, but have no impactful ministry throughout the other days of the week.

Where are the preachers when strategies are needed to redeem our community from the clutches of growing despair? My father, the late Reverend Orenzia Bernstine, served the dispossessed and disenfranchised people of Richmond for over 40 years. As a young preacher, I recall witnessing my father collaborating with other pastors to provide leadership in both church and city. They crossed denominational lines and political distinctions to give this city what it needed: a voice from those who were being largely ignored. I witnessed a time when nothing significant was ever attempted without including the voices of those who daily ministered to a significant percentage of the Richmond population. They did not have the academic privileges of many of us, but they were not intimidated by civic powers or community thugs. They viewed themselves as the necessary voices of reason, reconciliation, and redemption.

Presently, there is not a significant clergy organization worthy of the city's time or attention. There is no collaboration of clergy that commands and demands the respect of the community or civic government. The clergy in Richmond have seemingly abdicated the responsibility of community leadership, and by doing so, they have abandoned the people to figure it out for themselves, while allowing predators of every stripe to wreak havoc.

I know that my tenure here as a pastor has been short, but I have deep roots in the city of Richmond, and my long-time love for this city compels me to give voice to this constant concern. Where are the clergy?

We not only have an obligation and responsibility to respond to the mounting crises within our community, but we also have a wonderful opportunity to provide relevant leadership. We can be a voice in Richmond, and we can assist one another in making our city a real place of pride and purpose. We can be agents of change for the betterment of the community where our people live, work, and worship. We can proudly step forth and provide an answer for the query, "Where are the clergy?" Let them witness that we are here - loving, leading, and living out our call and convictions in the city we love, Richmond, California.

REFLECTION

1. Share your thoughts on the efficacy of the clergy in your community.

2. Can you describe a time when the clergy were visibly active in providing a voice in your community?

3. List the obvious obstacles preventing your community's clergy from providing a prophetic voice to community challenges.

4. Create a space and place where your congregation and/or organization can support the mobilization of a clergy-led community initiative.

APPENDIX

"THE CITY OF RICHMOND: WHERE VIOLENCE PIVOTS" *(A Historical Perspective of a Challenging Context)*

The brevity of this writing does not attempt to provide a detailed history of the city of Richmond, but I do want to offer a historical perspective that is grounded in solid historical data. I believe that what can be said about Richmond can probably be said about most cities in America, which is that the defining eras of the city were often responses to violence. Violence has served as the social pivot for much of what defines America, and also for Richmond. It could be said that violence is more American than apple pie, because apple pie does not originate in America. Moreover, there are many Americans who never tasted the sweetness of apple pie but have tasted the bitter bile of American violence. Richmond, however, clearly represents an American city that has pivoted on violence.

In 2004, the city of Richmond was cited as one of the most dangerous cities in America. I find this to be a rather infamous characterization for a city that once flourished in peace when occupied by the Ohlone Indians. Although the Ohlone Indians lived within distinct communities, of no more than 250 people each, they lived peacefully, shared strong community ties, and expressed deep spirituality through amazing arts. As is the dominant scenario throughout American history, European expansionism accompanied by militaristic interventions disrupted and destroyed the tranquil civilization of the Ohlone Indians. A rather interesting collaboration of corporate greed and Christian triumphalism led the Spanish excursions into the quiet shores of the East Bay, with no intention of including the demonized people known as "devils of the forest" .

Spanish explorers, Pedro Fages and Reverened Juan Crespi, were some of the first known European expansionists to visit the East Bay. The pivot from a tranquil Indian territory to a fledgling Westernized city happened through the violent uprooting of the Ohlone Indians. One writer noted that "European Americans never viewed the California Indians as being as assimilable as the Mexican population" . The argument continues that "California's white population retained the most barbaric claim one person can hold over another: the right to murder with impunity." Thus, the birth of Richmond began in violence and community disruption.

The liberation of Mexico from Spain, another violent initiative, set in motion the development of California. When large land grants were being awarded, the area soon to be named Richmond was carved from Rancho San Pablo in 1823 and given to Francisco Maria Castro, a former soldier of the Mexican army. After the violent Mexican-American War, Richmond began its journey into becoming a distinct Western community when State Assemblyman Edmond Randolph, from Richmond, Virginia, named the city of Richmond after his hometown. Richmond began as a humble settlement known as Point Richmond, and once boasted of having the world's largest winery in the community of Winehaven. The law-enforced violence of Prohibition forced the closing of Winehaven. Interestingly, many of the original buildings of the winery exist today as an eerie reminder of what used to be.

Richmond's emergence as an industrial community began with the coming of the railroad, an adventure led by Augustin

S. Macdonald in 1895. The history of the railroad is a well-known adventure of violence, characterized by forced labor, exploitation of Chinese immigrants and the violent displacement of Native Americans. Industrial growth escalated with the arrival of the Pullman Palace Car Shops, American Radiator, Standard Sanitary Company, Stauffer Chemical Company, and eventually, Standard Oil Refinery. Standard Oil Refinery, established by a known snake-oil salesman, became Chevron, currently the largest industry within Richmond. Ford Motor Assembly Plant and the Perilli Cannery added to Richmond's industrial vitality. During the 1920's, a strong Ku Klux Klan presence held violent sway over the policies and practices of the young city. The Ku Klux Klan influenced civic matters in Richmond to preserve assumptions of racial superiority with their classic maneuvers of violent intimidation. This served to minimize the African American presence and defined the city's community layout.

However, the war-time industry radically changed Richmond forever. I believe that no period of economic expansion matched the violent initiative of the war-industry period of World War II, 1940-1945. Richmond was at the center of the war industry and the activities of war indelibly reshaped Richmond. The need to build ships for the military triggered a massive migration from the economically challenged South into Richmond. Industrial whites and inspired blacks moved en masse to work the shipyards, and for many, to economically enhance the living standards of their families. It was during this time that my grandfather, McIntire "Mack" Miles, Jr., left Heflin, Louisiana, and moved with his family to become an intricate part of the Richmond community. In 1947, a young soldier from Bermuda, Louisiana joined his brothers in Richmond upon receiving an honorable discharge from the United States Army. That young man was my father, Orenzia Bernstine.

Although the war provided jobs for many migrating African Americans, Richmond was not a welcoming community. The population of Richmond nearly quadrupled (from 23,600 to 93,700) in three short years (1940-1943). The rapid and massive population growth placed a serious strain on limited housing, civic services and utilities. Consequently, decisions and policies were made that discouraged permanent housing for the burgeoning African American community. The influence of the Ku Klux Klan prompted the enforcement of segregated neighborhoods. Temporary housing was built for the incoming workers, but when the war ended, many of the housing complexes that were built for African Americans were quickly torn down. Interestingly, some of the housing built during this period remains, and represents some of the most violent neighborhoods in the city. The northern part of Richmond, which received the least amount of civic support, was one of the primary neighborhoods designated for African Americans. North Richmond remains one of the leading neighborhoods for gun violence and homicides related to young African American men.

An interesting development in Richmond was the creation of Parchester Village, "a development built in northwest Richmond in 1949, the first subdivision in the city where blacks could purchase homes." This community was built as a response to the lack of quality housing for African Americans, an initiative prompted by African American ministers, led by

Reverend Guthrie John Williams, pastor of the Mount Carmel Missionary Baptist Church. Reverend Williams brokered a deal with a white candidate for city councilman and land developer, Fred Parr, in exchange for the vote of the African American community. The councilman lost his re-election bid, but the housing development proceeded. The village itself is named after the white developer, but every street within the community is named after an African American clergy, one of which is Phanor Street. Phanor Street was named after the founding pastor of Bethlehem Missionary Baptist Church, Reverend Nathaniel Phanor. Parchester Village has often been a serious place of senseless violence among African Americans. A highlight of the city was a visit made by the Reverend Dr. Martin Luther King, Jr. upon invitation from the Reverend Booker T. Anderson, pastor of the Easter Hill United Methodist Church.

Richmond has influenced other significant developments, for instance, the influx of Asians. Asians now represent a significant part of the Richmond community, but the Asian presence in Richmond is also a response to violence – the violence experienced in their native countries. Vietnamese and other war-torn Asian communities have found their way to Richmond.

The present layout of the city was designed with the full knowledge that some communities were going to be isolated into pockets of poverty, and consequently, criminal responses would be inevitable. I can recall a community activist, Larry Greer, warning African American clergy that the planned construction of Highway 580 and the Richmond Parkway would devastate the existing African American communities.

Highway 580 and Richmond Parkway allow the commuting masses easy access to financial tributaries without ever laying eyes upon the poverty and violent-ridden communities that are consequently isolated. Although many new homes were developed within the surrounding communities - such as El Sobrante, Hercules, Hill Top, Marina Bay and others - the positive influences of those residents is minimal. Most of the people within those communities strategically avoid violence-plagued Richmond.

Although Richmond has developed a politically progressive constituency - such as being the largest city in the nation with a Green Party mayor, Mayor Gayle McGlaughlin - the challenges of the city remain. Richmond has become a leading city for the development of alternative energy and technology, recently being chosen as the site for the Lawrence Berkeley National Laboratory. Yet, the major challenge of Richmond remains the continuing gun violence and the accompanying response of massive incarceration. I consider both of these realities as being unacceptable and critical challenges to the relevance of the ministry of the African American church. I now turn to a brief historical perspective of the Bethlehem Missionary Baptist Church.

BETHLEHEM MISSIONARY BAPTIST CHURCH:
A Historical Perspective

The origins of Bethlehem Missionary Baptist Church began with urban congregations of migrating Southerners to California. Migrating Southerners, particularly African Americans, organized congregations out of social, psychological and spiritual necessity. Socially, upon arriving in California, the migrating African Americans were not surprised to find that white congregations in California were unwelcoming. Psychologically, they were dismayed by the fact that they were also unwelcomed by the established African American congregations. The emotional pain, of not being accepted by their own people, prompted the migrating African Americans to create their own spaces for spiritual sustenance.

Historically, black churches had been established in the Bay Area for years. Most of them were doing exceptionally well, in terms of providing spiritual sustenance and social support to the small, but established African American community. Congregations like North Richmond Baptist Church (organized by North Oakland Baptist Church), Beth Eden Baptist Church, Third Baptist in San Francisco, First A.M.E. and Bee Bee Memorial C.M.E. represented vibrant African American congregations in the Bay Area. "North Richmond Missionary Baptist Church was the first black Baptist church in Contra Costa County, and it became the most prestigious of Richmond's prewar church."

The black congregations that preceded the migrating Southerners had become socially acclimated to Western culture, and had shaped their ministries with a more learned and accomplished constituency of the African American community. As a result, many of the established parishioners viewed themselves as being different from their recently arrived brothers and sisters. For instance, "Richmond congregations and ministers were attacked by other congregations for being ' unsophisticated and too emotional'." The pastors of the established African American churches were often educated and seminary-trained. In addition, the memberships were made up of professionals, Pullman Porters, teachers, and others of assumed accomplishment. Consequently, just as there was race resistance from whites within the Richmond community and surrounding Bay Area cities, there was class resistance among blacks toward the untutored, unlearned, low-skilled migrants from the rural South.

An impassable obstacle to the assimilation of the recent migrants into the established African American communities was the relationship between the preacher and the people. For one, the polished style and cadence of the educated preacher failed to culturally connect with the rugged spiritual cadences of the rural-raised Southern Christian. Although many chose to struggle with the difficulties of being assimilated into the class-conscious established churches, most of the recently arrived migrants decided to establish congregations that better represented their rural roots. Another challenge for the recently arrived migrants was the inaccessibility of preaching opportunities for the rural-oriented preacher. Most of the established African American congregations resisted preaching opportunities, let alone opportunities for pastoral leadership, for the preacher who lacked formal learning and seminary training.

The frustrations caused by the inability of rural-rooted blacks to be spiritually connected, and the lack of accessibility to preaching opportunities for the rural-oriented black preacher, spawned the rapid birth of new congregations.

In an essay produced by Dr. J. Alfred Smith, Sr., he cited that there were three kinds of preachers in the Bay Area: 1) the learned preacher of the older established congregations; 2) the rural preacher who moved to the Bay Area at the request of the Southern migrants; and 3) the transformed quartet singers, who were literally encouraged or "called" to preach by the people, because their singing sounded like preaching. Shirley Ann Wilson Moore wrote that "some 'got the call' and became self-ordained ministers of the gospel." The Reverend Nathaniel Phanor seemed to have been carved out of the three fabrics of Dr. Smith's Bay Area preaching rubric.

Reverend Nathaniel Phanor never received formal training, but was incredibly charismatic and possessed amazing business acumen. He was a product of the Southern rural experience, thus he easily connected with the cultural idioms of the migrant community. He also possessed enough singing capacity to invite and encourage those who sang well. Moreover, he was a very gifted preacher who maximized the rural style that was so sought after by the migrating Southerners, particularly those from his home state of Louisiana, as well as Texas, Arkansas, and Mississippi. As a member of the Saint John Missionary Baptist Church, he was not given many opportunities to share his admirable preaching prowess, and was encouraged to consider starting a church. Thus, a Bible study was initiated in his home, which was also later held among the temporary housing built for the war industry workers. Like the Saint John

Missionary Baptist Church a few years earlier, the Bible study became the launching point of Bethlehem Missionary Baptist Church.

On April 8, 1945, at his home on 533 Spring Street, Apartment #1F, the Rev. Nathaniel Phanor announced, to a gathered mass of like-minded people, a God-originated vision to begin a church, which he named Bethlehem Missionary Baptist Church. Reverend Phanor shared the vision and the attending group accepted it. In compliance with California state laws for establishing a religious organization, a motion was offered by Reverend Herbert Guice and seconded by Reverend Robert B. Blackmore that Reverend Nathaniel Phanor would be the elected pastor of the newly-organized church. Both Reverends Herbert Guice and Robert B. Blackmore soon left and became prominent pastors in the Bay Area.

The Bethlehem Missionary Baptist Church began with twenty-two chartered members: Reverend Herbert Guice, Reverend Robert B. Blackmore, Reverend Curtis Ward, Reverend Levi Miller, Reverend Booker T. Payne, Brother Jewel Haynes, Brother Samuel Mitchell, Sister Frances Phanor, Sister Dorcas Haynes, Brother Allik Bernstine, Sr., Sister Millie Bernstine, Brother Allik Bernstine, Jr., Sister Lois Payne, Sister Lucile Blackmore, Sister Annie Thomas Ward, Sister Luala Bell, Sister Jessie Mae Ward, Sister Evelyn Ward, Sister Almeta Ward, Sister Ruth Marshall, Sister Willie Mae Macklin-Turner and Sister Dessie Bell Haynes. Of the 22 chartered members, only Sister Ruth Marshall remains alive and active in the Bethlehem Missionary Baptist Church. Brother Allik Bernstine, Jr. remains alive, but he is not an active member of Bethlehem.

As was the custom of the rural Southern church, a formal organization worship was scheduled and the charge to the church was given by Moderator Reverend G. W. Dowthard, pastor of Zion Hill Missionary Baptist Church in Richmond, California. There was an official call for letters from those who were seeking membership with the newly organized Bethlehem Missionary Baptist Church. The letters of membership from the Saint John Missionary Baptist Church were provided by the attending congregants, and the Bethlehem Missionary Baptist Church received as members the 22 chartered members. After the reading of the letters, the Eighteen Articles of Faith, Church Covenant and Hiscox Directory were adopted for congregational protocol by the group for the said church, and the right hand of fellowship was given to all the joining members.

A slate of officers was elected that clearly identified the church as having organizationally connected the people with their Southern roots. Organizationally, there was nothing radically different between the church "back home" and the newly established church in California. Bethlehem Missionary Baptist Church quickly captured the spirit and imagination of many of the Southern migrants, especially those who were connected with the families of the chartered members. One of those connected with the chartered members was my father, Orenzia Bernstine, who joined the migrating Southerners upon being honorably discharged from the United States Army.

Under the visionary leadership of Reverend Phanor, the vibrant energy of the young congregation surged rather quickly into considering a permanent home for the church. Property was purchased, and two months into its existence, on June 9, a groundbreaking ceremony took place. The first church building was built and a dedication service was held on December 9, 1945. The church experienced phenomenal growth, and because of the massive migration of Southern Blacks, membership reached a startling 1,169 people during the late 40's and early 50's. However, after the war ended and African Americans were discouraged from staying in Richmond, the number radically dropped to 285. It is rarely talked about at Bethlehem, and unknown to many of the current members, but many of us know that a reason for the drastic decline in the membership was a very public moral indiscretion of Pastor Phanor.

I suspect this may represent the first time that the Phanor indiscretion has been cited in a publication, but it was a major catalyst for a radical shift in the history of Bethlehem Missionary Baptist Church. It is noteworthy that the severity of the indiscretion was exacerbated by a gun being discharged during Sunday morning worship by an angry associate minister, who was the jealous husband of a suspected paramour. I know of this experience because I was present, and the preacher who pulled the trigger was a dear family member. I was a very young child, but I remember the incident vividly. My memory is made clearer by the fact that my father heroically intervened and averted a tragedy by grabbing my cousin's hand and pointing the discharging gun toward the ceiling. Reverend Phanor, consequently, was forced to resign and the young church struggled to find its bearing without pastoral leadership.

During the interim period, the associate ministers alternated in fulfilling the preaching responsibilities. It should be noted that from 1951 through 1956, seven lots were purchased. A kitchen and dining hall were added to the church, bringing the church's appraised value to seventy-five thousand dollars ($75,000.00). Yet, the departure of Reverend Phanor took a toll on the young church. Many members, disenchanted by the confusing internal struggles, left; some even formed splinter congregations.

After a very difficult period, a local pastor, Reverend Willie Lebeaux, introduced a young preacher. In April 15, 1957, the congregation was moved to call the young preacher as the next pastor. The preacher's name was Reverend Abraham Henry Newman, another Louisianan and former pastor of the First Baptist Church in Cairo, Illinois. Reverend Newman was somewhat of a learned preacher. He was vibrant, visionary, and methodical. He embraced a more structured approach to preaching and ministry, and demanded a more ordered and timely worship. He insisted on pew Bibles and hymn singing.

Unlike Reverend Phanor, who leaned heavily on charismatic spirituality, Pastor Newman transitioned the church into alignment with denominational structure. One of the things he did was to immediately organize a four-year leadership training course to train competent leadership for meaningful ministry. His passion and commitment to training leadership were initially met with resistance by those who had embraced the charismatic style of the founding pastor. As a result, many left and either started or became part of ministries that represented the familiar style of the rural-oriented church.

The transitioning of the Bethlehem Missionary Baptist Church accelerated when Pastor Newman led the church into building a new sanctuary, inclusive of a two-story educational complex. The multi-roomed complex was the first of its kind for an African American church in Richmond. Pastor Newman's vision of the new complex was received with external taunts and internal resistance. Area pastors and others did not see the relevance of a multi-roomed complex for a church, and some members within the congregation were resistant to the change. Without a consensus vote or majority decision, Pastor Newman personally secured a loan of $60,000 and the original church was demolished in September 1963, and the new building began.

Many of the men of the church rallied and assisted in the building, and an African American lumber company, Jones Lumber and Contracting, provided the lumber at a discounted price. In a little over a year, a new edifice was built and the educational complex was completed. Groundbreaking ceremonies were held on August 17, 1963. The edifice was completed on May 19, 1964. Dedication services were held on October 4, 1964. The completion of the edifice and educational complex furthered the transition of Bethlehem into a denominational, molded church.

Pastor Newman held leadership roles in every level of denominational work, and once served as the Chairman of the Board of Directors for the National Baptist Convention, USA, Inc. He served as President of the Richmond Branch of the NAACP, as well as a member of the Contra Costa County School Board. He was, without a doubt, one of the most influential church leaders in California, and a primary leader in the city of Richmond. He organized the Baptist Minister's Union in Richmond and provided leadership for Richmond clergy. Although Pastor Newman's influence was felt throughout the city, he preferred focusing on church renewal rather than social renewal. He favored the arena of the church over social engagement.

One of Pastor Newman's most visionary moments was when he led the Progressive Baptist Missionary Educational District Association in sponsoring my educational pursuits at Bishop College in Dallas, Texas. (While matriculating at Bishop College, I had the unusual privilege of serving as an assistant to Reverend Nathaniel Phanor, the founding pastor of Bethlehem Missionary Baptist Church.) Pastor Newman served Bethlehem for over 40 years, until his death in 2004. He sought to develop the congregation on solid Christian teachings and was known to say, "It takes inspiration and information." His legacy is that of a man who was ahead of his time.

In 2006, I was called to become the third pastor of Bethlehem Missionary Baptist Church. The church's membership had fallen below 100 active members, and the absence of young people did not bode well for the future of the church. Moreover, the community perception of the church was that it was not relevant. Based upon the challenges of the Richmond community and the state of the church, I accepted the challenge to transition a congregation to its next phase, which would revolve around the theme, "A Ministry that Saves Lives". I envisioned that everything we attempted would be, in some way, connected to the challenge of saving lives.

I have been blessed to build upon the momentum provided by both my predecessors, Nathaniel Phanor and Abraham Henry Newman. As a child of the church and preacher progeny of both my predecessors, I was welcomed as a son of the church. However, as one who had adventured away from the city and state for 27 years, inclusive of educational pursuits, I was viewed as an anomaly. Utilizing the people-orientation of Reverend Phanor and the ecclesial wisdom of Reverend Newman, I sought to transition the church into relevant ministry. Where Phanor emphasized inspiration, and Newman emphasized inspiration and information, I embraced the need for transformation. "Be not conformed to this world, but be transformed by the renewing of your mind." I consider my emphasis to be the logical next step in the evolution of the ministry of Bethlehem Missionary Baptist Church.

Upon arriving to serve Bethlehem, I was acutely aware of the need to empower the people for ministry. This was a daunting task, considering the authoritarian stronghold that had been held by Pastor Newman for over 40 years. One area of empowerment was the involvement of women in major leadership capacities, as well as opening the pulpit to women preachers. The latter was quite an accomplishment, given the staunch opposition to women ministers held by Pastor Newman. Nevertheless, the first woman was appointed to the Trustee Ministry and women were warmly received as ministers. Dr. Carole McKindley Alvarez, who was born and raised in the church, became the first woman trustee and now serves as Chairperson of the Trustee Ministry. She is accompanied by three other women: Glenda Roberts, Lisa Davis Lee, and Katrina Hamilton.

In less than six years, the Bethlehem church has become the leading congregation in social activism, and provides the most consistent presence in Ceasefire/Lifelines to Healing, an anti-violence initiative. In addition to the work with Ceasefire, Bethlehem has sponsored five H.E.A.L. (Help Educate and

Liberate) Conferences. The H.E.A.L. Conference is a collaborative with Contra Costa County College. It seeks to provide psychological and emotional tools for families and those involved with Foster Kinship Care. The School of Prophets continues the Newman tradition of seeking to equip ministers for more effective preaching and ministry. The current emphasis of the Bethlehem Missionary Baptist Church is to continue to do what the founding members sought: to provide a relevant ministry to people who are not always able to access normal social benefits. BMBC, as she is now referred to, seeks to provide a ministry that saves lives.

A MINISTRY THAT SAVES **LIVES**

NOTES:

www.ingramcontent.com/pod-product-compliance
Lightning Source LLC
Chambersburg PA
CBHW031250290426
44109CB00012B/520